IN DEDICATION

- To my brother, Jacob J. Ho... many.   Mr. ...

- To mother...her Christian example.   **Walter Herrick**

- To my mother, Nora S. Otto, who led me to the knowledge of Christ.   **Beryl Otto**

- To the memory of my beloved wife, Bunny Kartman **2001.**   **Paul E. Kartman**

- To my husband Elmer and two daughters, Dawn and Starr now with the Lord.   **Marjorie Cormican**

- To my wife, Sandy for **30** years of Blessing in Him.   **Ken Chin**

- **To my dear wife...my support for 55 years**.   **George Cocks**

- In loving memory of Alice Carpenter, devoted wife and mother.   **E.V. Carpenter**

- To my Mom, Dora Vaughn.   She fought the good fight, finished her course and kept the faith.   **Bev A. Vaughn**

- To my mother, Rachel Adams, who <u>never</u> gave up praying for me.   **Dick Adams**

- To my aunt, Willie P. Thomas, who made this gift possible.   **Artice M. Williams**

- To Carrie E. Friedline, my mother.   **Ray E. Friedline**

- To my grandson, William J. Rickards, III, who is an inspiration to everyone.   **Claire Biberich**

- To Son, Noah, who has shown superb ability to cope and retain his compassion.   **Martha House**

- To my daughter, Priscilla Coca, who exemplified her Christian faith in every way.   **Frank Coca**

- To the **NEW** me. #27   **R.J.G.**

IN DEDICATION

- **To Ron & Dawn Adkins...our son-in-law & daughter and to their five children...this book is dedicated.** As they go through life may they turn to Jesus Christ for the answer to <u>every</u> problem and circumstance.

KATIE Lynne / 11

DAWN and RON ADKINS

MITCHELL Dean / 9

LAURA
Dawn
13

MELISSA Grace / 15

AIMEE Rose / 11

HOW TO LIVE

Above

AND

Beyond

YOUR
CIRCUMSTANCES

SALEM KIRBAN

Published by **SECOND COMING, Inc.**
Copyright © 1974, 2004 by Salem Kirban.   Printed in the
United States of America.   All rights reserved, including
the right to reproduce this book or portions thereof in
any form.

ISBN No. 0-912582-01-4
Library of Congress Catalog Card No. 74-19641

DEDICATION/JESSICA

This book is dedicated to Jessica. She's just 4 months old. And her dad and mother, Wes and Doreen Frick, love her dearly!

And so do her grandparents! Doreen is our daughter. Jessica is our first granddaughter.

Jessica has Hemangioma, a benign tumor of the blood vessels.

Dear Jessica,
Right now as I look at your right eye inflamed and closed since three weeks after birth; as I see the swollen blotches on your face...to me and grandmom, and to your parents...**you are the most beautiful baby in the world.**

How often we have prayed for God to touch your tender body. Your lip is so swollen it is tender to the touch. And when you try to take your bottle, you cry. And our hearts cry with you.

We would be so willing to take this illness on ourselves, if it were humanly possible. When you talk to us (in your own little way) and when you smile and your one eye sparkles in recognition...we know it is your way of telling us that God wants us to live **above and beyond our circumstances.** And that's why this book is dedicated to you...dear Jessica.

Dear God,
You, in your providence, brought Jessica into our lives. Perhaps you knew we would surround her with an ocean of love. But as I write this I hear her pathetic cry in the living room. If it be Thy will, dear Lord, work Thy healing power in her body.

IN DEDICATION

When **HOW TO LIVE ABOVE and BEYOND YOUR CIRCUMSTANCES** was written in **1974** it was dedicated to our granddaughter, **Jessica Frick** who at that time was a little baby.   Shortly after her coming home from the hospital it was discovered she had a health problem called <u>Hemangioma</u> a benign tumor of blood vessels.   These appeared on her face and caused her facial profile to enlarge.   Both her mother, Doreen and husband Wes, prayed that God would restore her face to normal.   From age **4** to **14**, Jessica went through **7** cosmetic surgeries.   Today you would never know she had this affliction.   And she is blessed with a 4-year-old girl, Skylar.

JESSICA and SKYLAR in 2003

IN GRATEFUL ACKNOWLEDGMENT

To my wife, Mary
who upheld me daily in prayer as I wrote this book.

To my daughter, Doreen Frick
who devoted many hours to proofreading the text.

To Dave Koechel of Koechel-Peterson Designs
for providing an excellent cover design.

To Steven D. Husson of ULTRAGRAPHICS
for providing the film imaging prepress details.

To Dickinson Press for quality printing of this book.

IN EXPLANATION

This book covers **49** different problems covering every age group. While this book was originally written in **1974** the problems are even greater now in intensity than they were in the comparatively peaceful years of yesterday! It is our hope that this book will meet the need of all ages by answering their problems with practical solutions.

There are <u>four</u> pages devoted to each problem. The first <u>two</u> pages of each <u>four-page unit</u> show how a Bible character faced the problem. The succeeding two pages of each <u>four-page unit</u> show today's practical application to the same problem.

To survive, it is important today...more than ever before...to follow God's guidelines for **SPIRITUAL** prosperity.

WHY I WROTE THIS BOOK

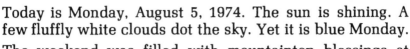

There is no better time than now to write this book. Why?

Because I need the advice I am about to write about!

Today is Monday, August 5, 1974. The sun is shining. A few fluffly white clouds dot the sky. Yet it is blue Monday.

The weekend was filled with mountaintop blessings at Montrose Bible Conference in Montrose, Pennsylvania.

But Monday brought me back to reality!

> The printer called...needed $18,000
> just when my current income was low.
> I called a man who had promised me a contract
> only to find he broke his promise.
> The bank made a mistake in our checkbooks.
> We called in two outside accountants and one bank
> employee. All three disagreed with each other!
> The Internal Revenue audited our books.
> And decided we owed them about $3000 more!

There's more...but I am sure you get the point.

What did I do? I could have sat down and cried...or worried. Instead, I got on my bicycle and rode around the block asking God to provide the answers and abundantly meet our needs.

And I'm leaving it there...at Jesus' feet. That's all I can do!

By the time this book comes out...God will have resolved these problems...and perhaps Satan will have thrown in a few more. Just because my books are doing well does not mean I am without problems.

My biggest problem now is how am I going to write this book...a book which deals with a subject I have never tackled before. How? I guess by taking one step at a time... writing one chapter a day.

The longest journey begins with a single step. I'm taking that step now. I hope my book, HOW TO LIVE ABOVE AND BEYOND YOUR CIRCUMSTANCES, will be as much as a blessing to you as it represents a real challenge to my own living.

Salem Kirban

Huntingdon Valley, Pennsylvania — September, 1974
Clayton, Washington — March, 2004

CONTENTS

Do you at times dislike school?

Congratulations! You have company! So did I!

One famous man wrote:

> I was happy as a child with my toys in the nursery.
> I have been happier every year since I became a
> man. But this interlude of school makes a sombre
> grey patch upon the chart of my journey.

That man's name was Winston Churchill who went on to become one of England's greatest statesmen.

But before you start feeling sorry for yourself why not first start counting your blessings. Suppose you had lived during the time of Christ. What would school have been like for you then?

In Palestine children at age five or six were required to go to school. The schools were held usually in the synagogues. Generally there were no seats as we know them today! Teacher and pupils either stood or sat on the ground in a semicircle. Up until 10, children were taught exclusively from the text of the Old Testament.

Children who skipped school were punished...often flogged. The children learned, as far as we know, chiefly through repeating by rote...from memory, without thought for meaning. The teacher would make a statement...then all the class would repeat it out loud. Memorization was the key to teaching. Then there followed hours of constant review.

Discipline was strict and the cane was often used. There were no ballpoint pens nor 3-ring notebooks. At one time pupils were given small wooden tablets covered with wax on which they copied passages from scrolls or sacred writings. Students wrote with a bone stylus pointed at one end and flattened on the other. The flat end was to erase the inscriptions and start over again. Can you imagine how dull life must have been without a Bic pen! Imagine some kid next to you kicking sand all over your wax notebook!

Benjamin Franklin once said of a man:

> *He was so learned that he could name a horse in nine languages; so ignorant that he bought a cow to ride on.*

Let's face it! Unless you are vitally interested...school can be a bore...but then, so is breathing. Yet it is necessary if you want life!

Even Jesus may have gone to school for a while as a child. But as Benjamin Franklin said, one can have all the learning in the world...but if you don't know how to apply it... it is a waste of time.

I flunked Algebra...had to take it over again in summer school. My biology teacher used to throw frogs at me. If one person did something wrong in class...the whole class got punished. Somehow...I got by and received a diploma with B's, C's and an occasional D thrown in. In fact I hated school so much, I went on to college (after a 2-year Navy stint) because I was told "you had to have a college degree to get a job."

Education is only a ladder...a chest of tools. Some of it may seem irrelevant (and quite possibly, is). But school, with all its inequalities, beats sitting at home doing nothing and getting into trouble. School is a transition period that helps you through the growing years of your life.

Then too, most people years later end up in jobs and professions which they never planned on in younger years. You may need that math, French, or English someday... because often what the 16 year old wants to do with his or her life is not what that same person will enjoy at 25 or 30! Thus a broad education is smart, like a life insurance policy. It will give you a wider selection years from now.

You don't have to like every course or every teacher. Some teachers can be very scholarly...yet dull. Every night tackle your most difficult homework *first*. And I know that this next statement requires the ultimate sacrifice on your part...but devote one hour on Saturday to studying the subject or subjects you are doing poorest in.

Learn good study habits. For unless you develop proper study habits now...your work habits in the future will be filled with problems.

Take history as an example. Suppose you have to learn a good many facts. I found it easiest to categorize the facts into easy-to-remember sections. Make your own simple outline on paper...for in writing you are aiding your memory.

Remember key words that unlock each segment of knowledge you must learn. If you were writing of President Nixon's second term...the key word could be WATERGATE. If you wanted to remember Marie-Antoinette...the key word might be CAKE. (It was said that when she was told the poor had no bread, she wittily quipped: "Let them eat cake.") In 1793 that unsympathetic statement cost her quite dearly. She lost her head in the French revolution.

First...break down what you have to learn into handy sections. **Second**...assign a KEY WORD or WORDS to each learning unit. **Third**...make your study assignment come to life!

And that may be hard...when you are studying the major rivers in Europe (who cares, anyway?). If there are 7 rivers, take the first letter of each river name. Try to make it into a word. That way, when it comes time to remember them... you remember the word...and every letter in that word stands for the first letter in a river.

And last, but not least, check your eating habits. What do you eat for breakfast? A bottle of soda, a cup of coffee, a doughnut? Stop right there! Your most important meal is breakfast! Eat a substantial breakfast...bacon, eggs, milk. Stay away from sugary cereals. Cereals like Product 19 or Total are more beneficial. Take at least a one-a-day type of vitamin at breakfast. And for school lunch...forget about french fries! And don't eat any sugary dessert. Try soup and a sandwich. White bread and pizzas will not help you. One step to liking school and making studying easier is to develop good eating habits. Why eat a poor breakfast and force yourself to feel lethargic during third period? Start right now! (To this day I don't know why that biology teacher kept throwing frogs at me!)

Idols worshipped in early Bible days by pagans included Athor, Tpe, Isis (goddess of fertility), Osiris (judge of the dead), Neith, Bubastis, Apis (the sacred bull), Beg (the hawk), Ibis (the crane), Shau (the cat) and Scarabaeus (the beetle).

You can be consoled by this fact...you are not the first one whose parents were not Christians.

Abraham, the founder of the Hebrew nation, had a non-Christian father. In fact in Joshua 24:2 it says:

...Terah, the father of Abraham...served other gods.

It is difficult enough living with a mother or father or both who are not Christians. But it becomes more difficult when those parents actively participate in a cult worship. Generally, if a parent is indifferent as far as any religion is concerned...they are more tolerant of others.

However, if a parent is active in a false religion...life at home can be difficult for others who do not go along.

Abraham's father lived in the Sumerian city of Ur, known in the Bible as Ur of the Chaldeans (Babylonians). This was in Babylon (now Iraq). When God called Abraham out of Ur...the entire family went to Haran (now in Turkey).

The "other gods" that Terah served were probably the gods of his city, a capital of moon worship. One god was called Sin...a deity connected with the regulation of time through the lunar month.

We do not know what problems Abraham faced in his youth in his home throughout his life. It was years later when Abraham was about 75 years of age that God called him and told him to move to Canaan. One thing we do know. Abraham did not allow his early pagan upbringing to deter him in obeying God.

And in spite of whatever problems he may have at one time faced at home, eventually they passed, and God chose Abraham to be the father of Jews. This covenant was made with Abraham while he was a Gentile. And he also became the spiritual father of all Gentiles in the faith (Romans 4).

Timothy, also, was the offspring of a mixed marriage. He had a Greek pagan father and a devout Jewish mother. Pagan Greece in those days offered sacrifices to idols to please their gods. Yet Timothy was fortunate in having not only a Godly mother but also a devout grandmother, Lois (2 Timothy 1:5).

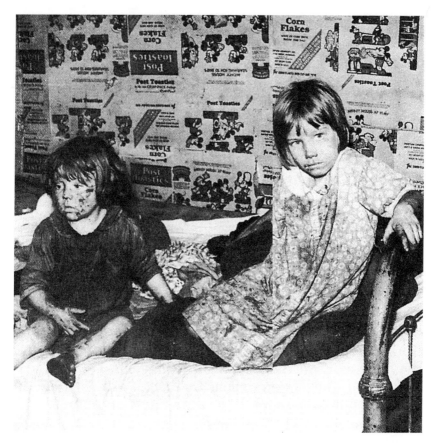

When you start feeling sorry for yourself at least be thankful you did not live during the depression days of the early 1930's. Many families lived in shacks made with makeshift walls of cereal boxes. It was not unusual to pay a $10 fee to earn $13.50. **Annual** earnings for a typist in those days was $624; for a waitress, $520. A registered nurse only made $936 annually and a dentist, $2,391.00. Teachers earned $1,227. About 25% of the labor force was unemployed.

At that time it cost $595 to purchase a Dodge, $585 for a mink coat, $1.79 for women's shoes, $18.75 for a vacuum cleaner, $10.95 for a two-wheeled bike, $2800 for a 6-room house and 29 cents for one pound of sirloin steak.

OK...so they are not Christians!

But let's look at the positive side of life. Don't be a pessimist. A pessimist is a person who blows out the light to see how dark it is. At least you can be thankful that you have parents! (After all, seriously, where would you be without them?)

I never knew my father. He died when I was about 2 years old. I was a youngster during the great depression years of the 1930's. We were so poor my mother saved Octagon soap coupons. I used to listen to the radio soap opera "Life can be Beautiful" and wonder if it ever would be for me. There was one advantage to being poor; it doesn't take much to improve your situation.

Let's assess the situation. Your parents will be in charge of your life at least till you graduate from high school. You have to decide to accept one of two courses:

    A. I'm going to give them a difficult time;
    B. I'm going to let my life be an example of real Christian living.

Now, you will have nothing to gain by giving your parents a hard time. It will simply mean headaches for both of you. And it is also unscriptural! The Bible says:

> *Children, obey your parents in the Lord, for this is right.*
> *Honor your father and mother, which is the first commandment with a promise,*
> *That it may be well with you, and that you may live long on the earth.*
>
>   *(Ephesians 6:1-3)*

God promises to honor your obedience to your parents. True, because they are not Christians, there will be inequities. Living with them may prove difficult. But, remember, God is able to help you overcome the difficulties. And you, by your personal Christian life...can be the means of winning your parents to Christ. And there is no greater joy for you...than the joy of eventually seeing them accept the Christ you not only love, but serve through your own obedient life of honoring your father and mother.

17

The Philistine archers overtook Saul and wounded him badly. Fearful that he would be captured and tortured, Saul took his own sword and fell upon the point of the blade. When his armor bearer saw that Saul was dead, he also fell upon his sword and died with him. See 1 Samuel 31.

Saul had a complex personality. He alternated between bursts of energy and fits of depression. He was moody and suspicious. Perhaps he was mentally ill? Yet he was a servant of the Lord.

Eli was a permissive parent. He was a weak judge and priest at Shiloh, a town in central Palestine where Joshua placed the tabernacle. He was a son of Aaron. It was to him that Hannah and Elkanah brought young Samuel to serve "unto the Lord" (1 Samuel 3:1).

Eli had two sons, Phinehas and Hophni. They too were priests. It was their custom to have one of their servants grab the sacrificial meat from the altars before it was even burnt for their own personal meals. Such an action was worthy of harsh punishment but their father, Eli only mildly rebuked them. His permissiveness finally led to the Lord allowing his two sons to be killed in a battle between the Israelites and the Philistines.

On the other hand Jonathan had an overbearing Christian parent...his father was Saul, the first king of Israel.

Jonathan had a dear friend, David. They first met after David slew Goliath and they became loyal friends. But his father, Saul, despised David because he realized David might replace him as King. His hate was so great that he told not only his servants, but also Jonathan, to kill David! Suppose your father told you to kill your best friend! That's exactly what Jonathan was instructed to do (1 Samuel 19: 1-7). Now while children are to obey their parents there are times when obedience is NOT to be given; that is, when such obedience would break the law or when such obedience would conflict with Scriptural teaching (Acts 4:19).

One day Saul was so angry at his own son Jonathan for not bringing David to him that he threw a spear at his son in a fit of anger (1 Samuel 20:33). Jonathan saved David's life by warning him of his father's intentions. But Jonathan also was faithful to his father. Both died in battle against the Philistines at Mt. Gilboa in the south central ridge of the Armageddon valley.

Eli was permissive and his children turned against God. Saul was oppressive yet Jonathan, through trials, became a rare jewel for God!

Life was carefree for me back in the summer of 1936 at Montrose Bible Conference. Seated (l. to r.) Lafayette Kirban, Stanley Maidment and Dennis Pryce. I'm in the center seated on the ground. I can remember often asking mother for a penny to buy candy. And how many times she had to tell me, "We can't afford it."

Now back in Montrose in the summer of 1974, with my wife Mary and our family, I can appreciate the problems my parents faced. And some of the things I did not understand then, I understand now. My wife is holding our granddaughter, Jessica.
▼

I went back in March, 1974 to my old homestead in Schultzville, Pennsylvania, with my brother, Lafayette (l.) The house was ancient when our family lived in it in 1936. Today it is a tottering wreck. Its weather-scarred wood and sagging roof were evidence it had seen better days. We paid $7 a month rent in those days, and it was a real struggle for my mother to meet the payments! ▼

The little young lady of the house, by way of punishment
for some minor misdemeanor, was compelled to eat her
dinner alone at a little table in a corner of the dining room.
The rest of the family paid no attention to her presence
until they heard her audibly delivering Grace over her
meal, with the words,

*I thank Thee Lord, for preparing a table before
me in the presence of mine enemies.*

Many young people do not realize how complicated life is
today for their parents. Its a project anymore just to buy a
postage stamp or order a pizza. You've got to fight traffic,
stand in lines, take a number. In my youth you could buy a
Hershey bar for a nickel. It weighed 1.18 ounces. By 1969
the weight dropped to 11/16th of an ounce. Then the price
went to 10 cents...then 15 cents and soon, 25 cents!

In this complex society, your father has the job of trying
to make ends meet. He's making more money than 10 years
ago but that money buys *less* than it did 10 years ago. With
every step forward it seems like he's taking two backward.
On top of that, just to get to work, he has to fight traffic
and higher costs. The days are long gone when a gallon
of gas was 31¢.

And your mother...she has less money to work with...yet
she has more demands on her money. Maybe her dress
looks a little out of style because she spent her last clothes
money on you—so you wouldn't look out of it. And there
are now more taxes to pay, to reduce even further her
ability to buy for her family.

Problems! You thought you had problems. How your mother
and dad wouldn't like to be back in school...care-free. No
obligations. No responsibilities of raising a family, paying
bills. That's probably why they seem at times impossible...
maybe a little irrational. Put yourself in their place.

Then, pray for them. Ask God to meet their needs...to guide
them. They are not perfect. Come to think of it, either are
you. Offer to help them in little ways, by doing the
shopping, mowing the lawn, doing the dishes. You'll be
surprised at the transformation...in both of you!

21

Now when evening came David arose from his bed and walked around on the roof of the king's house, and from the roof he saw a woman bathing; and the woman was very beautiful in appearance.

(2 Samuel 11:2)

For 40 years David reigned in splendor and power. As the height of his writing achievements he wrote the 23rd Psalm. "The Lord is my shepherd...."

Yet sometime after that his old nature influenced his life as temptations surrounded him. He slew seven innocent descendants of Saul (2 Samuel 21:6-7).

It was spring, about 994 B.C. David had sent the Israeli army to destroy the Ammonites. David did not go. He stayed in Jerusalem. Perhaps concerned about how the war was going, he took his troubles to bed with him. He couldn't get to sleep. So he went out for a stroll on the roof of his palace.

He looked over the city. Suddenly his eyes saw a woman of most unusual beauty taking her evening bath. Immediately he should have gone inside and got down on his hands and knees asking God to give him strength over the temptation.

But he didn't. He watched. And the more you watch...the better it looks. And Bath-sheba was indeed beautiful. But she was also someone else's wife! And David knew better. Yet he summoned her to his house. And she became pregnant with his child.

Now to sin once is bad enough...but David compounded his sin. He first tried to hide his sin by ordering returned from the war Bath-sheba's husband, Uriah...and when this failed...he had Uriah killed by ordering him to the front of the battle line. How could a man so righteous and so powerful within such a short time allow sin to control and ruin his life? The answer is easy. He took his eyes off God and directed his eyes to sin. For this David was to pay bitterly. His own wives had sexual relations with his son, Absalom, on the roof of the palace in view of everyone (2 Samuel 16:21-22). His son, Amnon, raped his sister Tamar (2 Samuel 13:1-14). Absalom killed Amnon (2 Samuel 13:23-29) and Absalom was slain in battle (2 Samuel 18:9-15). The seed of sin reaped a bitter harvest. Temptation commands a high price!

Temptations from without have no power unless there be corresponding desire within. Every temptation is an opportunity of our getting nearer to God. Temptation is sure to ring your doorbell, but you need not ask it in for dinner.

It can be perhaps said that today's young people face greater temptations than we faced as young people twenty or thirty years ago.

We are living in a fast-moving world. Social customs and standards have changed...unfortunately, for the worse. Yet young Christian men and women are expected to resist these more widely available temptations as effectively as we did in our days.

Pre-marital relations are now accepted by society as normal. No-marriage marriages are widely publicized by Hollywood. It's easy for anyone to see a pornographic motion picture rated R or X. One doesn't have to travel far to pick up magazines and books from the neighborhood adult bookshop. The Supreme Court can never decide just exactly what the definition of obscenity is...as a result the opportunities for sin come in like a floodtide.

Drugs are easy to come by. Suddenly, added to all this, our youth our exposed to the seamy side of government as leaders we respected go to jail for committing crimes. A President of the United States resigns. The world it seems is falling apart so why not enjoy life to the hilt.

Sin is fun...for a moment! Satan is smart enough to know people would not sin if they did not have pleasure in it. Sin is attractive. Sin is thrilling.

> Moses knew this yet when he grew up he *refused to be called the son of Pharaoh's daughter; choosing rather to endure ill-treatment with the people of God, than to enjoy the passing pleasures of sin; considering the reproach of Christ greater riches than the treasures of Egypt...(Hebrews 11:24-26).*

One secret of winning over temptation is to keep your eyes off of temptation and your mind and heart and spiritual eyes directed to God. Another secret is to avoid places where temptation will reach you. Then too, learn to say No early—when you can—so that you will not start or feed a sinful habit. Remember, sinful "fun" today...as in David's case...can bring you and yours horror and needless suffering tomorrow.

When temptation rears its attractive head, pull out your Bible and feed on the Word of God. Be sure to read 1 Corinthians 10:13.

> *Blessed is the man that endureth temptation; for when he is tried, he shall receive the crown of life which the Lord hath promised to them that love Him.* (James 1:12)

PETER

Peter was a man with many facets to his character. He was impulsive (Matthew 14:28), yet tenderhearted (Matthew 26:75; John 13:9). He became the spokesman for the twelve apostles and the initial leader of the infant Church after the resurrection of Christ.

Peter was a fisherman. He had no educational advantages. Yet Jesus chose him to be one of His disciples.

Many of us can relate to Peter...because Peter was inconsistent. He had his ups and downs. Sometimes he was brave. At other times he was a coward. Sometimes he exercised faith. At other times he was full of doubt.

Once he without hesitation drew a sword to defend his Lord. Yet, shortly after that, he denied his Lord to a servant girl.

He was the first to suggest a return to former occupations. Yet he was also the first to reach the Garden Tomb and realize that Christ had arisen.

In early 50 A.D. the Council of Jerusalem had met and decided that Gentiles should not be burdened with the yoke that Jews had to bear and be under the Mosaic law. No longer should Jewish and Gentile believers be separate. They should fellowship together.

Yet Peter at Antioch hesitated between the challenge to conform or not to conform. He was enjoying the company of Gentiles. He even ate with them. Then the big news was announced that James was sending a delegation to Antioch and Peter started to waver (Galatians 2:12).

He decided it best that he no longer eat with his Gentile Christian friends. He made this decision because he was afraid what the Jewish legalists might say...those who still insisted that circumcision was necessary for salvation.

Paul rebuked Peter for his indecisiveness and his desire to conform to the demands of the legalizers. Galatians may have been written before the Council. Like Peter at Antioch, the Galatians too were so anxious to conform that Paul addressed the Galatians in strong words: "O foolish Galatians...Christ has redeemed us from the curse of the law... For ye are all the sons of God by faith in Christ Jesus" (Galatians 3:1,13,26).

Paul opposed Peter when he found Peter more desirous of conforming to please people rather than pleasing God.

The Red Chinese are a good example of what occurs when an entire nation conforms to the orders of one man—Chairman Mao. The children are taken away from their parents at a very early age to state-run schools. They are taught to conform. They dress alike. Then when they get older they all conform by learning the art of military warfare. One day 200 million of them will march toward Israel!

Remember, real Christianity demands dedication and devotion. And most Christians are not ready to make such sacrifices!

During the long, painful years of the Vietnam War we were faced with great upheavals in society.

Young people who blamed the war on adult leaders suddenly decided that the way problems could be resolved was *not* to conform. Seeing that "Middle America" was always well dressed...many young people decided to look as bedraggled as possible. Boys became like girls and let their hair grow in long curly locks. In fact, it became difficult to distinguish between a boy or girl.

School leaders found themselves unable to enforce their dress codes. While people were dying all over the world some parents (with nothing better to do) and children staked their life on the length of hair and even took their issue to court. As time went on those young people who did not want to conform...found in the very act of not conforming...that they actually *were* conforming. For any young boy with a haircut and well dressed actually became a non-conformist and quite a rarity.

This wave of non-conformity next led to open sin. It was the new gospel of Yippies and Hippies and free love. The television networks gave them big play and the leaders of these networks will have to answer to God for the countless thousands of youth sent down the drain by their influence. Rock concerts became the "in" thing, and anyone who was anybody conformed to the parade of sin.

A Christian must realize that there are times when he or she should conform and other times when they should not conform. The answer should not be based on whether "everybody else is doing it." That certainly does not make it right. Just because some churches allow young boys to wear shoulder-length hair and some "Christian personality" adults follow...does not make it right. Just because some churches introduce music that imitates the world does not justify your accepting such in your life.

Your decision in each case to conform or not to conform must be based on the question: "Is it Scriptural? Is it really honoring God or giving way to the flesh? Does it represent real sacrifice on my part that will be directed to winning lost souls to Christ?"

29

John Mark had problems.

His mother's name was Mary. Acts 12:12 speaks of the house that Mark lived in as "...the house of Mary, the mother of John who was called Mark...." Quite possibly Mark's father was dead and in growing up did not have the guidance that a father could provide.

From the description given of the house and the fact that they had a Greek slave (Acts 12) it can be safely suggested that Mark's family was a family of wealth. They were zealous Jews dedicated to serving Jesus.

Mark's cousin was Barnabas, also apparently a man of means (Acts 4:36,37). Barnabas accompanied Paul on his missionary journeys. Mark had accepted Christ through Peter's influence (1 Peter 5:13). Barnabas invited Mark to accompany him and Paul to Antioch as an "attendant." See Acts 13:5. Antioch was the home of many leading Christians and this must have proved a thrill to Mark. Imagine the thrill you would have if some impressive personality invited you to travel with them on an evangelistic tour!

Mark apparently became disenchanted on Paul's first missionary journey. Quite possibly he became homesick and having been suddenly thrust in the limelight...was confused as to what direction to take. Also it must be remembered that Mark came from a strict Hebrew family and it is quite possible he objected to the offer of salvation to the Gentiles on condition of faith alone. When Paul and Barnabas went by ship to Pamphylia in Turkey, Mark left them and went back home.

When it came time for Paul's second missionary journey, Paul refused to take Mark with him. This caused friction. Barnabas then left Paul and took his cousin Mark to Cyprus (Acts 15:39).

Not until about 11 years later do we hear of Mark again (Colossians 4:10). He is at Rome *with Paul*. The conflict of former years has been resolved. And in fact, Mark is one of the faithful few Jewish Christians who stand by Paul. Paul now calls him a "fellow-worker" and a great "comfort" to him. In 2 Timothy 4:11 Paul asks Timothy, who is at Ephesus, to come to him, and to pick up Mark along the way for he is "useful for ministering," so useful that his ministry is a joy to Paul's heart.

Mark, through personal trials, had finally found direction for his life!

As a young person, remember not to be impatient. Sometimes it is difficult to determine what direction you would like your life to take, particularly in your early married years. Tomorrow's horizon may seem like a restless sea. I was 42 years of age before I realized God's will for the remainder of my life...writing books. If you are reading this, and are over 40, don't give up hope. Life can begin at 40!

Our daughter, Diane, in the summer of 1974, decided to devote her summer to reaching children for Christ. She took a training course with Child Evangelism...then became a summer missionary. Going from community to community she conducted Bible classes right on the lawn. That summer she reached 334 children, and 48 accepted Christ as Saviour and Lord. It was with joy in her heart that she entered her senior year at high school knowing she had invested her summer wisely and was setting the groundwork for direction in her life.

Most great men want to be remembered in history as having accomplished some important task. To them they strive today so they can appear in the history books of tomorrow.

President Richard Nixon was such a man. Time after time he expressed concern that history would remember him as a man who brought peace to the world and made it possible not only for this generation but also future generations to live in peace. Yet on 9:04 PM on August 8, 1974 he became the first President of the United States to resign from office under the threat of certain impeachment because of obstruction of justice. His farewell remarks included:

As a result of these efforts, I am confident the world is a safer place today...This, more than anything, is what I hope will be my legacy....

President Nixon's goals were high, but his direction was partially misplaced.

Too often young people who were dedicated to Christ...go to a Christian college...graduate...and then suddenly lose direction for their life. They end up in a secular life six or seven days a week and their goal has become a desire for worldly recognition or gain.

First...in order to find direction for your life make sure you look to Christ as your Guide.

For thou art my rock, and my fortress; therefore, for thy name's sake lead me, and guide me.

(Psalm 31:3)

Second...remember your calling. Has God called you to be a missionary? If so, don't become a bank teller and settle for second best. Don't be concerned about material gains for yourself or the name you will make for yourself in history.

Direct your energies and your life, whether it be in a secular job or full-time Christian work, to honoring Christ and becoming a productive servant in winning and edifying others by your witness. See Ephesians 5:15-20.

Salome, with silver tray in hand, awaits the execution of John the Baptist, so she could present his head to her mother, Queen Herodias.

One man said:

> Men think highly of those who rise rapidly in the world; whereas nothing rises more quickly than dust, straw and feathers.

The entire Herodian family history is one of fighting, suspicion, intrigue and shocking immorality.

Herod the Great ruled from 37 to 4 BC, and used subtle flattery as did his father to achieve a prominent place in society. He was so determined to be successful and accepted...he even murdered his wife and his sons. He robbed his own people in order to bestow gifts on the Romans. And one of his last acts was to give an order to execute another of his own sons.

Herod Antipas was the son of Herod the Great. At his father's death he became ruler of Galilee from 4 BC until 39 AD. He was a superstitious man (Matthew 14); cunning and wholly immoral (Luke 13). Herod Antipas forfeited his prestige among the Jews when he married his niece, Herodias—who was already wed to his absent brother.

When John the Baptist pointed the finger at Herod Antipas for sinning by sending his wife away and marrying his brother Philip's wife...Herod had him cast into prison.

It was Herod Antipas' birthday. A state dinner was being held. Herod's new wife, Herodias, was furious at John... wanted him killed...but Herod recognized John as a man of God. But Herodias had a plan. Her young daughter danced a dance in front of Herod and his men. She was so sensational that Herod said:

> ...Whatever you ask of me, I will give it to you; up to half of my kingdom.   (Mark 6:23)

Her mother told her to ask for the head of John the Baptist on a platter. And Herod...with such a burning desire to be accepted among his dinner guests...would not refuse. His desire for acceptance outweighed his desire to do what was morally right.

Herod was to be stripped of his power in later years and died in exile.

Cars and young people seem to go together. In this way new friends are made. Even many adults spend thousands of dollars to compete in "street nationals" in hopes of recognition. Yet, as a Christian, your desires should be primarily directed to those things that have eternal values.

Do you ever notice how some people are name-droppers. They love to be associated with important people.

Look at any church and you can find those who are seeking status either by becoming the head of some committee or the head usher, an elder or a deacon. Even churches sometimes, knowingly or unknowingly, have a class system. Sometimes this begins in the young people's fellowships and many a young person is treated as an outcast because his social standing is not up to theirs.

There's an old Chinese proverb that says:

> *He who sacrifices his conscience to ambition*
> *burns a picture to obtain the ashes.*

And many times, those who strive to be accepted, compromise their own Christian life and testimony to achieve this end.

God does not command of you to be accepted in this world. In fact He reminds you that:

> *...In the world ye shall have tribulation...*
> > *(John 16:33)*

Nor should you waste your time trying to win the approval of others, even those in your own church. Certainly you should be cordial and sincerely concerned about the spiritual and physical welfare of every member of your church. But you should not waste your time trying to climb a social ladder of acceptance in your young people's group, your fellowship society or in your church. If you do, then you are misdirecting your energies as a Christian.

Proverbs 18:24 reminds us that:

> *A man of many friends, comes to ruin, But there*
> *is a friend who sticks closer than a brother.*

Remember, your rewards in Heaven will not be determined on how many friends you had, but how you invested your time in serving Christ.

The Israelites were oppressed by the tyrannical demands of Pharaoh. They built two treasure-cities, Pithom and Raamses and labored in every variety of public work. Pharaoh, angered because they were multiplying, commanded his people to throw the male infants into the Nile.

God through Moses led His people out of this bondage and oppression. Then in the wilderness, the Lord provided their every need. Yet, the Israelites, forgetful of God's redemption, made a golden calf and began worshipping it.

The life of Moses, in some ways, parallels the life of Christ. He was born when an edict was out to kill him. He spent years in obscurity. His own people scornfully rejected him. He redeemed Israel in her darkest hour.

He had a decision to make...whether to be "called the son of Pharaoh's daughter" (Hebrews 11:24) and live a life of ease or return and serve his people. He chose the latter. And it meant a lonely job as a shepherd...forty years of wandering in the desert of Midian. Moses may have wondered many times whether he had made the right decision...but God was preparing him for bigger things. In fact, Moses becomes one of the central figures of Scripture, mentioned some 720 times in the Bible.

VOCATION

When Your Job
Gets You Down

Moses had everything against him. The Pharaoh, fearing the exploding Israeli population, ordered that all Hebrew boys were to be killed as soon as they were born.

Through God's protection, Moses was spared and grew up in Pharaoh's household. He was educated in Egypt's culture. Wealth, advantage, position, comfort, prestige... he had all of these as a member of the King's court. Yet his job got him down...he could not forget his Hebrew heritage and that his own people were suffering as slaves.

Moses had the job of leading the Hebrews out of Egypt. But he had two fears...the fear of failure. Moses was afraid because of his slow speech that he could not be such a leader. The other fear was his *fear of man.* He feared that people would not listen to him. Criticism seemed to unnerve him and he felt too small to accomplish the task.

But God went before. Moses led the people across the Red Sea, accompanied by miracle after miracle from God. In the middle of the desert...they had water. In the evening God provided meat; in the morning, bread. But the people complained. They remembered the days of bondage in Egypt when they had cucumbers, melons, leeks, onions and garlic (Numbers 11:5). Moses was at the end of his rope. Complaints, complaints...that's all he heard. Calling on God he exclaimed:

> Why, hast Thou been so hard on Thy servant?
> I alone am not able to carry all this people...If
> thou art going to deal thus with me, please kill
> me at once...
>
> *(Numbers 11:11,14,15)*

Moses' job had finally got to him...so much so, he was willing to die to escape the pressure of leadership.

Under Pharaoh he had an ideal job...all that anyone could ask for...but his conscience made him uneasy. Under God he became the leader of his nation...but the problems brought him to the verge of nervous collapse! He was to see the Promised Land but never to enter it.

When your job gets you down, imagine having to raise your family on an old Chinese junk floating in the garbage-strewn Hong Kong harbor! Then, consider how fortunate you are. Reassess your values. Perhaps the job you now consider so important may, from an eternal standpoint, add up to nothing but chaff. Don't waste a lifetime doing something you don't enjoy.

One of the greatest warriors for God was Moses. He had the best job the world had to offer...and was not satisfied. God commissioned him to deliver his people from bondage. He had the best job the Lord had to offer...and yet he found it surrounded with problems.

There is no such thing as an ideal job. Every job has its headaches. Imagine having a job which became so unnerving that you would ask your supervisor to kill you. That's exactly what Moses requested!

People often work at a boring job all their life looking forward to the day they will retire. When that day comes... when they have nothing to do...many soon die. It is not an uncommon thing to read of people dying one or two years after retirement. There is no more goal in life...no routine... no purpose.

Most people hold on to a job...regardless of how unhappy they are...because they want security! Security does not buy happiness! I have seen people fill their life with conflict, plagued by illness, all because they wanted security and wanted to keep up with their other friends in their church social set.

For 42 years I wandered in the wilderness not knowing what I really wanted to do. In the first 5 years out of college I probably had about 7 to 10 different jobs. I remember, when jobs were hard to get, I sent a resumé to the Presidents of 50 different companies. I remember getting an interview with the President of Stetson Hat Company... while other job applicants were waiting in line to see the personnel officer. I didn't get the job, however, because— I didn't wear a hat!

But, if you are dissatisfied with your job...don't be married to it because of security. Send out job resumés directly to the company President. Then, too, consider serving the Lord. You may be poorer...but happier. I remember a wealthy manufacturer of toys. He had money but he was not happy. He gave it all up to serve the Lord in South America as a missionary. He died recently after spending about 15 fruitful years on the mission field!

When Christ came to earth He could have claimed all the material wealth of the world, for He owned "...the cattle upon a thousand hills" (Psalm 50:10). Yet he devoted His time to serving others and finally died so that we might have eternal life. Would you be willing to follow Christ to the cross? Where do your priorities lie?

In Christ's day, there were some very wealthy people. Many of these wealthy people achieved their gains by being very hard on the poor. They led a luxurious kind of life, spending in one day more than a laborer could earn in a year (some still do that today!). Their wives dressed lavishly and bedecked themselves with jewels. They had the costliest of perfumes.

Some wealthy people, like Joseph of Arimathaea, were good men. Most of the rich acquired their wealth from land ownership or trade. When the Jews sent a delegation to complain of Herod to Augustus...one of their chief complaints was that he had acquired extensive real estate holdings (to their disadvantage) and that he had over 60 million dollars in gold! Many high officials made their fortunes through bribery.

Martha, the daughter of Boethos, bought the office of high priest for her second husband, Simon ben Gamala, for about $10,000. Even in current history we have read about allegations that wealthy men have been able to buy ambassadorships by donations to a political party. In fact, wealthy Martha insisted that a carpet be unrolled for her every time she went to the Temple.

The rich young ruler of Luke 18:18-23 asked Jesus how he could get to Heaven. This young man had secured all the material possessions he wanted. But these did not bring him peace of mind or peace of heart. Jesus was aware that this man was outwardly a good man who obeyed the commandments of not committing adultery, nor killing, nor stealing, etc. This young man also assured the Lord he had kept these commandments. But Christ wanted positive devotion...not simply a negative devotion of keeping certain laws.

Jesus told him: (1) Sell all you have, (2) distribute your wealth to the poor and (3) come and follow me. This the rich man could not do. It is difficult for a man of wealth to accept discipleship!

In what direction are you traveling down life's highway? Don't wait until the sunset years to take an inventory of your life. Then all you can have is a lifetime of regrets. An obsession for material possessions will never bring you happiness and will serve to draw you away from God.

"Seek ye first the kingdom of God and His righteousness, and all these things [life's necessities, not life's luxuries!] shall be added unto you" (Matthew 6:33).

There are actually today some religious personalities who are preaching both on radio and television the Gospel of Wealth. They slip in Bible verses, occasionally, and usually out of context, to try to convince their listeners that Christ meant for all Christians to abound in material possessions.

Some faith healers publish reports showing that when people gave to their ministry they "paid off their mortgage," "got a new car," "bought a boat," etc. These religious personalities exude success in their ruffled shirts, Italian silk suits, expensive shoes, diamond fingers, big cars, and entourage of fellow-travelers who worship the ground they walk on.

One television personality proudly admits he drives in $30,000 and $40,000 cars. He tells people his message is not one of "pie in the sky by and by" but riches now on earth. If you follow his advice of positive thinking he tells you, "You can't lose with the stuff I use!" Many gullibly follow him.

If you have a desire for material possessions you should spend one evening with your wife and a sheet of paper before you. Divide it into two sections. On one side list the material possessions you already have. On the other side list the material possessions you want. Then...count the cost of what you want.

Then ask yourself the question...after you get all these things you want...will they bring you happiness? Will they mean your life for Christ will be more dedicated? Will they mean you will spend more time serving Him or less? A friend of mine wanted a recreational vehicle. Finally he purchased a $20,000 Dodge Travco mobile home vehicle. It had everything...a kitchen, a double bed, a shower and toilet, a living room, air conditioning and stereo radio. But it did not bring him happiness. In fact it served to cause him problems and he became concerned about the misplacement of his priorities. Realizing his mistake he disposed of the mobile home, and his family is happily serving the Lord.

Jonah was so deep in a rut that he failed to change course
when God directed him to go to Nineveh. It took drastic
action on the Lord's part to steer Jonah in the right direction.

Jonah was in a rut.

But he liked the rut he was in. Someone once said "a rut is a grave with both ends knocked out."

God had other plans for Jonah. He commanded Jonah to go to Nineveh. Nineveh was one of the most ancient cities in the world, founded by Nimrod. Nimrod was a great-grandson of Noah. Nineveh was located in the country now known as Iraq.

Nineveh was named after a god, Nina, and it was filled with temples. It was primarily an Assyrian city and its people were proud and war-like. One Nineveh ruler sacked 89 cities, captured 208,000 prisoners and killed young and old alike. Another's reign was described as "...a bloody mess of war after war, siege after siege, starved cities and flayed captives." This one ruler placed the head of a rival king on a pole in a garden where he and his queen were having a party. He then bled a general to death like a lamb.

It was to Nineveh that God directed Jonah to go. But Jonah was in a rut—instead he took a ship in the opposite direction to Tarshish (probably southwestern Spain). He disobeyed, the account indicates, because he feared the wicked people of Nineveh would hear God's message and repent, and then he would be a fool for having preached threats and judgment. Then, too, Nineveh had persecuted his people for so many years. He was unwilling to be a missionary to a people for which he had nothing but bitterness!

But God placed him in the belly of a great fish...to turn Jonah around. This time Jonah obeyed. He took God's message to Nineveh. The people of Nineveh repented in sackcloth and ashes. And God spared the city! See Jonah 3.

This made Jonah angry. He had predicted Nineveh would not repent. Jonah felt perhaps that he was called only to preach to the Jews. But God's message extended to the Gentiles as well. There were 120,000 people in Nineveh. Yet, their salvation did not make Jonah happy. He never learned to get out of the rut of his small world.

This is the house I grew up in...located in Schultzville, Pennsylvania, a few miles above Scranton. It would have been very easy for me to get in a rut. But circumstances pushed me out of this home that I loved. If someone had told me then that at 42 years of age I would give up a career in advertising to start writing books...that I would travel around the world at least 4 times...I would not have believed them! But with God's direction, I got out of the rut. I had never written a Cantata before either. But one day I decided to ask God to give me direction and I sat down and wrote the 1 1/2 hour Cantata...**DAY OF JUDGMENT.**

Pictured on the left is Rev. Joseph Dunets. As a boy he grew up in New York in the midst of deprivation and heartaches. God brought him out of a rut and sent him across the U.S., where for the past 26 years he has been a Pastor in Portland, Oregon. And every year, he pays his own way overseas to preach for an entire month in South America, Africa or Asia! (Also pictured is Mary Griffin, a lifelong friend from childhood days, and our son Duane. And, oh yes, that's our daughter Dawn photographing the cat!)

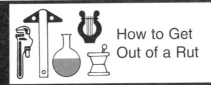
Gerald Rudolph Ford, Jr. had one ambition...to become Speaker of the House. But God had other plans for his life. He became Vice-President in 1973. And on Friday, August 9, 1974 he became President of the United States. His son supplied him with a Bible opened to his favorite verse:

Trust in the Lord with all thine heart,
And lean not unto thine own understanding.

In all thy ways acknowledge Him, and He shall direct thy paths.

(Proverbs 3:5-6)

Jonah was aware of God's plan for his ministry but refused to follow it. Jonah was in a rut.

Many people are in a rut because they do not heed the message of the Psalmist "Show me thy ways, O Lord; teach me thy paths" (Psalm 25:4).

The key word here is *"thy."* Oftentimes we are guilty of planning our own life...mapping out OUR path and doing it in OUR way. As Christians we should seek HIS path and follow HIS way.

Then, too, many Christians find themselves in a rut from an employment standpoint. They do the same job day in and day out. On Saturday and Sunday their pattern of living is the same...it never varies. Sunday always pot roast... Monday always hot dogs. Life becomes dull and meaningless. It has lost its vibrancy.

My first job was in the insurance business. I found it dull, without challenge. My next nine jobs were working under somebody else. I found this very restricting and unimaginative. Finally, I went out on my own.

Jonah's entire horizon was limited to Israel. To him, nothing else existed. What about you? Has life become a routine bore? Then, perhaps it is time you should trust God and step out. Together, you and your mate, should seek HIS WAY and HIS PATH and live triumphantly for Christ!

Jacob yearns for beautiful Rachel as he takes care of the flocks of her father, Laban.

There was a family feud. Jacob tricked his father, Issac, by wearing goat skins. Isaac, almost totally blind, not realizing he was tricked imparted the first-born's blessings to Jacob.

Rebekah, knowing of Esau's vow to kill Jacob urged Jacob to go on a long journey and search for a wife.

The long dusty trail ended at Haran in Southern Turkey by a well. Here he spotted a very beautiful girl...Rachel. He was soon to discover that Rachel was his cousin.

In Old Testament times marriages were arranged for young people by relatives. Marriage could take place as early as eleven or twelve. And the wife was paid for, just as though she were a piece of property. Generally there was no preliminary courtship. Love, if love existed, was to come after marriage, not before.

Jacob spent seven long years working as a dowry to pay for Rachel. The day of the marriage came. The bride, according to oriental custom, was heavily veiled. When Jacob awoke in the morning imagine his shock when he discovered his new bride was not Rachel...but Leah. His uncle Laban explained that "It is not the practice in our place to marry off the younger before the first-born" (Genesis 29:26).

Laban suggested Jacob wait until the bridal seven days was over and he could marry Rachel too after the week...if he would work another seven years (Genesis 29:27-28). Jacob did just that...and within one week he had two brides, Leah and Rachel.

Two brides within one week produces conflict. And while Jacob was deceived by his uncle, he no doubt often remembered how he had deceived his own father by pretending to be Esau.

Leah was not a "Miss America." From all indications, however, Rachel was a natural beauty...much to be desired. Quite possibly not only Laban but also Leah believed she would never get married. But God works in mysterious ways. Leah not only got married, but was more fertile than Rachel bearing for Jacob six sons and a daughter...sons who were to be the foundation of the 12 tribes of Israel.

Sunday school picnics and other Young People's fellowship socials and meetings are good ways to develop lasting friendships that may eventually end in a happy marriage. Such friendships often begin in the early teens.

After man came woman, and since then some say, she has been after him ever since.

It has been said that marriage begins when you sink in his arms and ends with your arms in the sink.

It takes two to make a marriage, someone else has quipped —a single girl and an anxious mother.

Marriage is the high sea for which no compass has yet been invented. Getting a husband is like buying an old house. You don't see it the way it is, but the way you think it's going to be when you get it remodeled.

We are living in a day when young men are conditioned to look for outward Hollywood beauty in marriage. This leaves many eligible young girls, who may not be a Marilyn Monroe, wondering if they will ever get married.

But as a young Christian girl, remember...don't be in a hurry to get married...for if you choose the wrong partner, because of your impatience...you will have an entire lifetime to repent! It would be good for you to read 1 Corinthians 7:32-35,38.

If after prayer you feel the Lord is calling you to have a mate through life...then prepare yourself. Dress attractively but modestly. Always be cheery on the outside even though you may be crying on the inside. Ask the Lord to work in the man who one day will be your husband and direct his heart to yours. And to help him along...a little perfume may get his head turned in the right direction.

Above all, let your mate-getting activities be centered in Christian circles. Don't make the mistake of believing you can go with an unsaved boy and change him later. It doesn't work! Satan will tell you it does. But it doesn't. I met my wife, quite by accident at a young people's fellowship. Above all, never lower your Christian standards to get a boy. If it is God's will that you get married...God is able to provide the boy in His time. If it is not His will, your life will be more vibrant, more productive for Christ as a single woman. If you leave it in God's hands...all things will work together for good.

There are many Bible illustrations showing that marriage to an unbeliever is sin. Ezra, at the water gate, rebukes the Israelites for disobeying God and urges them to repentance.

The Lord warned Moses that the Israelites should not compromise with those who were idolators. Because they were idolators they worshipped other gods, friendliness with them, the Lord warned, would cause Israel to find themselves accepting their daughters as wives for Israel's sons. See Exodus 34:12-17.

Then, your sons will commit adultery against me by worshipping their wives' gods. God warned that His people must have nothing to do with unbelievers.

And in Deuteronomy 7:3-4 God further warned the Israelites that when they finally entered the Promised Land:

> ...you shall not intermarry with them [the unbelievers]; you shall not give your daughters to their sons, nor shall you take their daughters for your sons.

> For they will turn your sons away from following Me to serve other gods; then the anger of the Lord shall be kindled against you, and He will quickly destroy you.

The Israelites, however, disobeyed and subsequently the 12 tribes of Israel began to be scattered and the 70 years of Babylonian captivity ensued. Ezra, a leading priest of his day received permission from Artaxerxes, king of Persia for the Jews to return to Jerusalem in 458 B.C. What rejoicing as the Temple was rebuilt and dedicated (516 B.C.). But then, once again the Jewish people drifted into apostasy, marrying heathen neighbors.

Ezra, dismayed, called for a special 3-day meeting. The meeting was held on a street "...that was before the water gate" (Nehemiah 8:1). Ezra read God's Word to the people, pointing out their sin of marrying unbelievers.

The people, realizing they had disobeyed God, signed a covenant, which included the promise that they would not marry outside of their fellowship of believers (Nehemiah 10:30). Remembering Solomon's sin of intermarriage, the Israelites asked God to forgive them and to guide them.

When you are in love with someone who is not a Christian you find it very easy to justify your position. Yet, inwardly, if you know the Scriptures, you know you are wrong...that it will never work out!

Outwardly, to your parents and loved ones, you maintain a positive attitude of "Our situation is different. He (or she) is a good person...clean living. And he doesn't mind my going to church after we're married. In fact he promises to go with me and he will allow me to bring our children to Sunday School."

You may perhaps take a different approach. "I believe I can influence him and lead him to Christ after we are married. I don't want to push him now to a decision or I will turn him away from the things of the Lord."

The above are all perfectly reasonable and plausible answers. **And they are all inspired and directed by none other than Satan!** If you, as you are reading this paragraph, find yourself in exactly this circumstance...the above sentence will make you angry. That's just what Satan wants!

You say you are in love...and when you are in love, reason goes out the window. God made man and woman differently. He designed them as magnets that would be physically and psychologically attracted to each other. Once a man gets into the magnetic field of a woman...there is a drawing power that desires union. Quite, understandably, when you are in love you feel that it is a deep abiding love—"He loves me for what I am." Realistically, however, initially your love of each other contains a large degree of the love of one physical body to touch and possess another physical body. (If you don't believe this...try developing a love relationship with your sweetheart **without** touching each other!)

God tells us in many portions of Scripture that marrying someone who is an unbeliever is wrong! **It can never, never be justified.** And it will usually lead to a life of misery! To refresh your memory, read the previous page on how Israel suffered. God reminds you: "Be ye not unequally yoked together with unbelievers; for...what communion hath light with darkness? And what concord hath Christ with the devil? Or what part hath he that believeth with an infidel" (2 Corinthians 6:14-15)? Remember, "...to him that knoweth to do good, and doeth it not, to him it is sin" (James 4:17).

This is one problem where there is no question, according to God's Word, as to what the solution is — **stop dating the non-Christian friend!** And don't accept a "shotgun salvation" either. Oftentimes, someone anxious to marry, will accept Christ at the counselling session a few weeks before the wedding. Fine...then hold off for six months and be sure that person is real, not a counterfeit.

God is testing you. For if you shed your non-Christian friend, He may have in the wings, a dedicated Christian with whom you will experience real Christian love that is both lasting and fulfilling!

Rachel, anxious to bear a child by Jacob, asked Leah for the mandrakes.

Imagine that your husband not only married you, but that he also married someone else the week before he married you!

Here he is with two wives. Of course there would not be one jealous bone in your body. *All* the bones would be jealous.

And suppose from your husband's union with his first wife this wife became pregnant again and again and again and again...and four children were born! But you could not produce one!

Well, that's exactly what happened to Rachel. Leah was fruitful from Jacob. Rachel was barren even though she was very beautiful.

Rachel was in a rage and she screamed at Jacob:

> *Give me children, or else I die*
>
> *(Genesis 30:1)*

Now that's getting pretty dramatic. In fact, Rachel was so anxious for children she arranged for her servant-girl, Bilhah to substitute for her with Jacob. Bilhah produced two children.

It was wheat harvest time. And Leah's son, Reuben, found some mandrakes in the field which he gave to his mother. Mandrakes were a tomato-like fruit which were believed to arouse sexual desire. It was called the "love-apple."

Rachel asked Leah for the mandrakes. She promised her that if Leah would give her the mandrakes "...he [Jacob] may lie with you tonight" (Genesis 30:15).

Leah went out to meet Jacob and said:

> *...Thou must come in unto me; for surely I have hired thee with my son's mandrakes. And he lay with her that night...and she conceived, and bore Jacob his fifth son.*
>
> *(Genesis 30:16-17)*

So Leah became pregnant...without the magic of the mandrakes. And Rachel also conceived...with the mandrakes (Genesis 30:22,23).

Remember the joys of your childhood and how your eyes lit up when the Thanksgiving turkey was brought to the table!

In a controlled group of infertile couples...surveys showed that only 35% of this group were hopelessly sterile. The balance were physically capable of having children.

About one in six of all marriages is sterile.

Although most males would want to believe otherwise, it is as frequently a deficiency in the husband that causes the sterility as in the wife.

Just because one cannot conceive in the first two years of marriage does not necessarily indicate sterility.

You may be familiar with those who have tried for years to have children...then in desperation adopted a child...only to find that within a short time the wife became pregnant. This relaxation of effort on the part of husband and wife often produces results.

If it is your desire to have children and you find yourself, after three years of marriage, unable to produce a child, you should see a doctor. Oftentimes hormone therapy with women is successful. Both you and your husband should determine whether it is physically possible for you to conceive.

After making the above determination...then relax. Don't carry your problems to bed with you. Remember, they will still be there when you wake up...so commit all the day's activities and tomorrow's problems to God. Then forget about them. Ask God, if it is His will, to honor your union with children. Then, leave it in His hands.

If your physical union cannot produce children then seriously consider adopting a child. In 2 Kings 11:1-3 we read where Jehosheba, sister of King Ahaziah of Judah saved Joash from certain death by adopting the little boy at a time when Athaliah, daughter of Jezebel, was determined to kill him.

After a proper and pious upbringing, Joash served God as a great ruler.

By adoption, your Christian influence on that child may chart for him a life of dedicated Christian service! You can meet a child's need—and the adopted child can meet yours! And, don't listen to any old wives tales, many of the most attractive and well balanced children today are those who were adopted.

Tamar had lost her first husband, a man whose name was Er. The Bible said that Er

> ...was wicked in the sight of the Lord; and the
> Lord slew him.   (Genesis 38:7)

According to Old Testament law (Deuteronomy 25:5);

> When brothers live together and one of them dies
> and has no son, the wife of the deceased shall not
> be married outside the family to a strange man.
> Her husband's brother shall go in to her and take
> her to himself as wife and perform the duty of a
> husband's brother to her.

Er's brother was Onan. Both were wicked men, and sin apparently had made them bitter enemies.

Yet when Er was slain by the Lord, it was Onan's duty, under Mosaic law, to marry Tamar, his brother's wife... and from that union conceive a child so that the family property would remain within the family and that the dead brother's name would live on.

But Onan was so bitter against his deceased brother that he did not want a child born through his efforts to carry on Er's name instead of his own. (It was the custom for the one first born to carry on the dead man's name, and not his own father's. See Deuteronomy 25:6-10).

Judah turned to his son, Onan and commanded him:

> Go in to your brother's wife, and perform your
> duty, as a brother-in-law to her, and raise up off-
> spring for your brother.

But Onan rebelled. Genesis 38:8-9 tells us:

> And Onan knew that the offspring would not be
> his; so it came about that when he went in to his
> brother's wife, he wasted his seed on the ground,
> in order not to give offspring to his brother.

Because of this sin, God slew Onan also. Actually Tamar was denied a child by a rightful husband three times but finally gave birth to twins by her father-in-law. Tamar's name is recorded in the ancestral line of Jesus (Mt. 1:3).

As food prices become higher and shortages exist, many parents find it almost impossible to feed their present families adequately. Shopping is just as difficult in Jerusalem, pictured here, as it is in the United States.

Studies both in England in the United States indicate that women who take the "pill" run a risk of blood clots as much as 11 times greater than non-pill users. Women who take the "pill" are nine times more likely to suffer the most common type of stroke than nonusers according to a report by the Collaborative Group for the Study of Stroke in Young Women. Although doctors still consider it safe, women who take the "pill" run a small risk of developing some serious side effects.

Presently in the United States there are some 215 million people. Our doubling rate is now about every 30 years. By the year 2000 there will be some 400 million living in the U.S. Red China has 800 million. By the year 2000 they will have 1 billion, 600 million. The doubling rate of India, Africa and South America is every 12-15 years. This certainly would be a good argument not to have children.

But the Bible suggests that a Christian husband and wife should strive to have children. Psalm 127:3-4 reminds us:

> *Behold, children are a gift of the Lord;*
> *The fruit of the womb is a reward.*
> *Like arrows in the hand of a warrior,*
> *So are the children of one's youth.*
> *How blessed is the man whose quiver is full of them.*

If you and your husband are physically capable, you should strive to have children.

Now there does come a time when additional children may endanger your physical or mental health. And after the age of 40...while it is possible...many physicians will suggest that child-bearing may bring more complications than would occur in the 17-35 age bracket.

How to prevent additional pregnancies? There is of course, the pill. Millions of women in the U.S. and throughout the world are taking them, but doctors caution on their prolonged use. And their after-effects can cause serious disease and death. Then there is sterilization for men, vasectomy. But this, too, I would not recommend as it can have serious physical and mental after-effects.

One of the simplest measures of birth control with what apparently are the least after-effects is a laparotomy operation performed on the woman. It is a simple operation... can be done as an out-patient, within a few hours. It is sometimes called "belly-button" surgery. A small incision is made in the belly button. A slender instrument, a laproscope quickly seals the Fallopian tubes, preventing further pregnancy.

Joseph Conrad once said: "Being a woman is a terribly difficult trade, since it consists principally of dealing with men."

Michal, King Saul's daughter, loved David. Perhaps she and David met each other quite often when David came to see her brother Jonathan.

Saul despised David so he used flattery by telling David he would like to have him as a son-in-law. Saul said David could have Michal. But David replied: "...I am a poor man ..." (1 Samuel 18:23).

David knew he could not pay a dowry for Michal. So Saul replied:

> The king does not desire any dowry except one
> hundred foreskins of the Philistines...
>
> (1 Samuel 18:25)

David not only fulfilled Saul's wish but he and his men came back with 200 foreskins! (Remember—Israel was at war with the Philistines at this time.) So Michal became David's first wife. Michal became distraught at her father's attempts to kill David and helped him escape from a window one night. To cover his escape she made a stuffed image and put it in David's bed. The ruse gave David enough time to escape.

With David in exile and away from Michal for a long time it would be almost impossible for a healthy marriage to exist. It appears that some years passed before David and Michal ever met again. In the meantime David had married Abigail and then Ahinoam of Jezreel. When David became Saul's successor as king, he asked Michal to return to him. She did. She saw David marching up to Jerusalem with the ark of the Covenant accompanied by 30,000 men of Israel. When she saw him wearing only plain white linen and leaping and dancing before the newly restored ark...she was angry. She was angry because he had removed his royal robe and danced in plain garb like a simple priest. This lowering of the King to mix with the commoners angered the daughter of Saul, still filled with the pride of "royalty."

In scorn she screamed:

> How the king of Israel distinguished himself
> today! He uncovered himself today in the eyes of
> his servants' maids as one of the foolish ones
> shamelessly uncovers himself!

(2 Samuel 6:20)

From then on Michal despised David. Although, in the interim she had married Phalti, she had to leave him and follow David (2 Samuel 3:16). The marriage between David and Michal ended up not a happy one and Michal died bearing no children (2 Samuel 6:23).

Do you remember when you carved her initials in a heart on a tree? The same love you had then should be even greater now. It should be a love that is so encompassing that it becomes blind to her faults and aware of yours.

Impossible marriages are usually the result of impossible personalities.

One statesman said: "To make a good marriage, the husband should be deaf, and the wife blind."

And a Chinese statesman said: "Marriage in China is like putting a kettle of cold water on the fire. Soon it is boiling and stays hot. But in the West, marriage is like putting on a cold stove a kettle of water that is boiling tempestuously — but presently cools off."

The word "marriage" is derived from *maritus*, which, in turn, is derived from Mars, the god of War. Metropolitan Life Insurance Company, in a survey, discovered that the more children a couple has the greater chance of the marriage surviving. My ABC's of a happy marriage are:

(A) Acknowledge Christ as your Saviour and Guide;
Accept His example as your example for life;
Appreciate the fact that you, as well as your mate, are far from perfect.

(B) Be blind to the faults of your wife (or husband);
Be in prayer daily for marriage harmony in your life;
Be aware of your own shortcomings and do something about them.

(C) Call together on the Lord by prayer, on your knees together, whenever a problem arises;
Communicate always with each other—silence is not golden;
Consider that you are united as a temple of God.

And stay off of junk foods and sugary snacks. Unknowingly they can cause erratic behaviour. Sugars contain virtually no food value...can put you on a roller coaster of peaks and valley living and interferes with the absorption of proteins, calcium and many other minerals necessary for good health. This can contribute to a problem personality.

Be sure to read 1 Peter 3:1-12. Wives should be submissive to their husbands and by their godly lives be a witness to their husband. Husbands are in turn commanded to be loving—understanding, kind-hearted and humble in spirit.

After the prophet Nathan told the story of how a rich man,
who had many flocks, took the sole lamb from a poor man...
David was angry at the rich man's selfishness. At that
point, Nathan pointed his finger at King David and said,
"You are the man!"

David had sinned and any attempt to justify a wrongdoing
simply complicates the situation. Sir Walter Scott wrote:

> Oh, what a tangled web we weave
> When first we practice to deceive!

Bathsheba was a very beautiful young woman, and we can assume that she had a very appealing body. Her husband, Uriah, was one of King David's most trusted generals. It was evening. Bathsheba was on the roof-top of her home bathing. This was the custom in those days to bath on one's roof. What she should have realized was that her roof was plainly visible from King David's palace.

David, having spent a restless day, concerned about the present war, could not get to sleep. He decided to take a walk on his palace roof. He spotted Bathsheba. Physically she was probably very attractive and David was immediately attracted to her. David sent messengers and commanded that she come to him.

The law commanded that she obey her king...for a woman in those days was completely subject to a king's will. And she did obediently come.

> *...and when she came to him, he lay with her...*
> *And the woman conceived; and she sent and told*
> *David, and said, "I am pregnant."*
> *(2 Samuel 11:4-5)*

For David, the web of sin enmeshed him into further sin and great sorrow. David eventually had Bathsheba's husband, Uriah, killed by placing him in the front of the battlefield.

David paid dearly for his sin. God, through the prophet Nathan, told him what his punishment would be:

> *...the sword shall never depart from your house...*
> *I will even take your wives before your eyes, and*
> *give them to your companion, and he shall lie with*
> *your wives in broad daylight.*
> *(2 Samuel 12:10-11)*

Then David's first child by Bathsheba died. After, this in the following years trouble followed trouble as the prophet's word of judgment bore its fruit in David's life. We here learn that no one—not even a King David—can sin against God with impunity.

Marriage is much like a ship. Young love, like a ship at the pier, experiences no storms. But when marriage sends the ship of love out to sea, sometimes the storms appear overwhelming. If the Saviour is the Master of your ship, you will sail through the storms and emerge as stronger Christians!

Many books and motion pictures have been written on the so-called "seven-year itch."

Unless a husband and wife are fully dedicated to the Lord it is very easy to take each other for granted. Then after the full flush of the sexual aspects of marriage are experienced...many an unstable person then seeks variety. Men, in particular, as they reach the age of 38-48 sometimes feel their physical powers are slipping away from them and seek reassurance through another younger mate. Some, however, fall into sin at much earlier ages, and no one age can be looked at as the age when one may most easily fall.

There is no doubt that sin is attractive. And the human body of the opposite sex is attractive. There is a compelling magnetism there...created by God for a purpose. And that purpose is only to be culminated in male-female union in marriage...not before. Then after marriage that union is only to be with your wife (or husband)!

Yet misplaced eyes and desires can lead a mate astray. Suddenly he or she finds one self in love...but with someone else! And it is not a figment of one's imagination. Your partner is really in love. It is a physical, sensual love. But nevertheless...this love occupies one's entire being. One who could rationally think before...suddenly thinks irrationally. One who was a stable Christian before suddenly twists Scriptures to justify his or her action.

When this happens...don't criticize your mate. Don't abandon him. But PRAY. Pray for your mate and also pray for his new-found love. Pray that God will not give them one minute of peace until they see their sin and rectify that sin. The most difficult thing for you will be to show love for your mate. Don't be overbearing but do remind him that you love him dearly. You are not going to give him up. God, through marriage gave him to you and you are praying that God will resolve this temporary testing of your mutual love. Continue to live with your mate but avoid sexual relations until the problem is solved. Be sure to look in your own life as well during this testing time to see whether some of your habits should not be changed to make you a sweeter, responsive Christian.

Abigail quickly rode out to the desert to intercept David, apologizing for her husband's behaviour.

Abigail could be considered one of the wisest women of the Old Testament. Abigail was both intelligent and beautiful but her husband, Nabal was "harsh and evil in his dealings" (1 Samuel 25:3).

At the time of this incident, David was a shepherd who was hiding from Saul in the wilderness of Paran near the Sinai desert. David had about 600 followers and they voluntarily protected the flocks of many of the herdsman in the area from thieves. One of the flocks they protected was that of Nabal's, who had 3000 sheep and 1000 goats.

It was sheep-shearing time. Nabal was having a feast and drinking quite heavily. David sent ten young men to the feast (as was the custom) to ask for a little food from the banquet table. After all, David and his men had protected the sheep from many thieves and not once had stolen any sheep for their own food. It was a polite and customary request.

Nabal, in his drunken stupor, cried out:

> Who is David? And who is the son of Jesse? Shall
> I take my bread and my water and my meat...and
> give it to men whose origin I do not know?
>
> (1 Samuel 25:10-11)

David was furious...so furious that he and 400 of his men put on their swords and were determined to kill all the men in Nabal's camp. Abigail heard of David's intentions and quickly got 200 loaves of bread, two barrels of wine, five dressed sheep, two bushels of roasted grain, 100 raisin cakes and 200 fig cakes and went into the wilderness to intercept David. She apologized to David for the bad-temper of her husband. David was deeply moved and told her to return home in safety.

Returning home she found her husband still drunk. The next day Nabal had a stroke. In ten days he died. When David heard this he asked Abigail to become his wife. She became one of David's eight wives. She was humble and gentle—David potentially willful and temptestuous. Undoubtedly she had the greatest influence of all wives in helping David learn patience.

My friend and associate, Bob Conner, is the most even tempered person I have ever worked with. He and I both take 30 vitamin pills a day! Perhaps that is the secret. (I must confess, however, that I sometimes become impatient.)

Perhaps Bob's secret lies in the toasted cheese sandwiches and the special fruit drink concoction that my son Duane has whipped up for him just before Bob retires for the evening!

There is more evil in a drop of sin than in a sea of affliction.
And every time you lose your temper you advertise your-self. A man's temper improves the more he doesn't use it.
Thomas Jefferson wrote:

> When angry, count ten before you speak; if very
> angry, a hundred.

In this complicated world...it is easy to get frustrated, and angry. We are so prone to computerize everything...take a number to get a haircut, take a number to get waited on, fill out a number to be admitted to a hospital. We are treated now as numbers...no more as individuals who have names...so Christians can easily become righteously indignant when their valuable time is squandered in a waiting room of some doctor or dentist. I often say that Christians should exercise grace (then I go on to say, "My grace expires after 5 minutes").

I become very impatient with inefficiency. Yet one must learn to control one's temper...and when a word has to be said, to say it in love and use that opportunity to win a person to Christ.

If you lose your temper quite often you are falling into Satan's trap of diminishing your Christian testimony. Check your eating habits. This may be a clue to your frequent outbursts to temper. Are you eating regularly? Instead of three big meals a day, try eating 5 small meals daily. Stay off of sugary desserts, candy bars, ice cream. Take a daily vitamin supplement. These measures may help you. And the next time you find yourself getting angry...try getting angry while at the same time repeating silently to yourself

I LOVE YOU in the Lord!

Also, go to your local health food store and buy a stress supplement vitamin combination (generally containing the B and C vitamins).

(Now where in the world did I put my pencil. Duane...did you take my pencil again? Why take my one pencil? I bought you a whole box of them!)

Paul reminds the Corinthians that their spiritual gifts should be used to glorify God and to win others to Christ.

Corinth was a very important city. It occupied a strategic geographical position. Ships, to save time in going around the southern capes of Greece would stop at Corinth. Here their cargoes would be hauled across the narrow isthmus on a wooden track and loaded on another ship on the other side.

Corinth was a city of wealth, luxury and immorality. The phrase "to live like a Corinthian" meant to live a life of immorality. Their greatest goddess was Aphrodite, the goddess of love. Her temple had 1000 priestesses of vice.

Paul founded the Church at Corinth on his second missionary journey. He spent a year and a half here in the home of Priscilla and Aquila. Because of the sin in the city, even the church that Paul started had problems.

Many people in Paul's day were becoming very proud of the spiritual gifts they possessed especially in such a city as Corinth. Paul had told them that spiritual gifts included: wisdom, knowledge, faith, the gift of healing, the effecting of miracles, the gift of prophecy, etc. (1 Corinthians 12:8-10.)

Many Corinthian Christians were using these gifts as ends in themselves...showing off their superior righteousness. They forgot that if God gave them a specific gift...it was not to make them proud...but that they might use that gift to glorify God and to win others to Christ.

As a result, many in Corinth who were dedicated Christians, but had no specific attention-getting gift, were looked down upon by their fellow Christians. They were in a city filled with sin...yet they felt like the fifth wheel...unloved and unneeded.

Paul, realizing that the sin of pride dwelled in his congregation, reminded them in 1 Corinthians 12:22-27 that those thought to be the least important are really among the most important...if one suffers...all suffer. He reminds them that the body of Christ is not one member, but many. Everybody cannot be a preacher, a prophet, a teacher. But each, regardless of station in life, are part of God's body. The street sweeper is important to Christ as is also the evangelist, Paul. Each is needed. For each, Christ died!

In 1974, returning from a 14-day speaking tour in Minnesota, this sign designed by our daughter, Dawn, was waiting for me in the driveway.

It's a wonderful feeling to be needed. I remember when I came home from an Around-the-World 30-day trip in 1970. I walked up to the patio and saw this large sign welcoming me home. Shown left to right are Doreen, Diane, Duane, Dawn, my wife Mary and our daughter-in-law, Eileen.

I have witnessed many Christians wasting their life away because they felt they were not needed.

Perhaps part of the fault lies with our modern evangelistic techniques. Popular religious television shows feature big name personalities...famous singers, football players, actors and actresses who may have accepted Christ but have not necessarily dedicated their life wholly to serving Him sacrificially. It would be most unusual to see the janitor of the evangelistic organization on a TV special!

Yet Jesus Christ tells us through Paul that the janitor or secretary is just as important, if not more important, than the big-name evangelist or Hollywood star turned Christian.

I have been around many so-called top name Christian personalities. Some I have found have feet of clay who have allowed the pride of position to make them feel they are more important than the lowly grandmother who is eking out an existence on Social Security.

Whenever I have spoken whether it be in a Church, a school or a Bible Conference, I have always made it a point...regardless of how tired I was...to stand at the door and personally shake hands with everyone who passed by.

Unfortunately, this is the age of Christian "Stars." In each church you can find those who esteem themselves of a higher and more important social class than others. This is sin. They would do well to read Philippians 2:3-4:

> *Do nothing from selfishness or empty conceit, but with humility of mind let each of you regard one another as more important than himself;*
>
> *do not merely look out for your own personal interests, but also for the interests of others.*

How can you feel needed? First, remember...Jesus Christ says you are important to Him. You are so important that He died for you! In light of this, serve Christ not to get the accolades or recognition of men. But, rather, whether you feel needed or not, serve Christ solely because He loved you and promises to fit you with a crown of recognition eternally in Heaven.

Today's counterpart of the Pharisee could be the Hasidic
Jew. They are the very strict orthodox Jews who practice
absolute adherence to the Law. They are easily recogniz-
able by their mode of dress as seen in this photo.

We read in Job 27:8-9 the question:

> For what is the hope of the hypocrite, though he hath gained, when God taketh away his soul?
>
> Will God hear his cry when trouble cometh upon him?

In Christ's day there were three prominent societies of Judaism — Pharisees, Sadducees and Essenes. The Pharisees were the most influential.

The name "Pharisee" means "the separated ones." They were the religious leaders of the Jews who practiced strict adherance to the Law. They wore distinguishing garments that set them apart from others. They accepted the Old Testament Scriptures, but as time went on they bitterly opposed Jesus and His teachings and His claims of Messiahship. Christ condemned them because of their theology and life of legalism.

Directing his remarks to the Pharisees Christ says:

> Beware of practicing your righteousness before men to be noticed by them; otherwise you have no reward with your Father who is in heaven.
>
> When you give alms, do not sound a trumpet before you, as the hypocrites do in the synagogues and in the streets, that they may be honored by men...But when you give alms, do not let your left hand know what your right hand is doing; that your alms may be in secret; and your Father who sees in secret will repay you.
>
> (Matthew 6:1-4)

The Pharisees, like actors acting under a mask, literally sounded trumpets under the pretext of calling the poor. But in reality they just wanted to make sure that when they gave money in the offering there was a crowd to see them.

Discriminating Christians must realize that not everything about the Pharisees was bad, but this fault of constantly seeking public recognition was one that the Scriptures do call to our attention.

A mother soon learns that the needs of her baby must come before her own needs. Our daughter-in-law, Eileen, makes sure Darrell has his bottle before eating her own dinner at a recent family gathering.

It is human nature for us to want to hear the praises of men. We sometimes get offended if the Pastor passes us without saying hello, or if we fail to get recognition in the Church, from the pulpit, for participating on some committee.

But we must keep foremost in our mind the fact that we should shy away from the praises of men.

Oftentimes in Church we are asked to pray for "Mrs. Jones who had a heart attack" or "Mr. Smith who just lost his job."

But prayer alone can be cheap. We as Christians should put wings to our prayer and give...but give in secret. Why not visit the Hospital Administrator in the hospital where Mrs. Jones is and pay one week of her hospital bill... anonymously without anyone knowing it? Why not go to the supermarket and see the Manager and pay for $25 or $50 worth of groceries anonymously for Mr. Smith? This is giving in secret. But God who sees in secret will reward you openly. Learn to sacrifice for others...in secret.

Perhaps in your own personal life you have had financial reverses. Perhaps certain problems in your life are causing you to alter your life style.

Don't be sad about these problems. Don't fret about them. Either God is able to meet your every need or He isn't able. If you are firmly rooted in the Word of God you realize that in everything that comes your way, you should give thanks (1 Thessalonians 5:18). God *is* able to meet your every need.

Don't be like the Pharisee, wanting the whole world to see your works...but, rather, quietly and in secret, live an exemplary Christian life helping others who are in need, whether physical or spiritual. And in so helping others, and perhaps making real sacrifices, you will find that your own life will be more enriched and meaningful.

What were to you sacrifices will soon become opportunities. Soon the race for materialism...the blowing of your trumpet...will be supplanted by the thrill of serving Jesus!

Because of her faithfulness, her bowl of flour was never exhausted nor did her jar of oil become empty.

Ahab was the seventh king of the northern kingdom of Israel. He was a strong king. It is believed that he commanded 2000 chariots and 10,000 men. But his greatness vanished when he married Jezebel, for Jezebel introduced to Israel Baal worship and licentious orgies and killed many prophets of the Lord. Because of Ahab and Jezebel's sin, Elijah the prophet announced that Israel would be punished with a drought (which ended up lasting for three years and six months).

An obscure widow woman, living at Zarephath (now in Lebanon), was suffering because of the effect of the drought which had now been in effect 2½ years. All she had between her and her son was a handful of meal in a barrel and a little oil in a cruse. Her face reflected the agony of despair in her plight.

The prophet Elijah faced a similar situation. But God had sent him to the brook Cherith...one of several brooks that empties into the Jordan river. He drank from the brook and ravens brought him bread and meat both morning and evening. One day that brook dried up.

Here was a widow woman with her little boy on the brink of starvation. Into her life suddenly walks Elijah tested of God seeking something to eat. Where does he, of all places, request food? From the widow woman! He asked her for water. She started to look for some. Then while she was looking he asked her for bread. To the widow woman it was an impossible request!

Tearfully she unburdened her soul: "...I have no bread, only a handful of flour in the bowl and a little oil in the jar; and behold, I am gathering a few sticks that I may go in and prepare for me and my son, that we may eat it and die" (I Kings 17:12).

But Elijah had faith. He asked her to bake the bread and give the bread to him. Imagine, this poor widow of Zarephath, taking her *last* morsel of bread and giving it to *someone else!*

And because of her faithfulness to a prophet, throughout the drought, the bowl of flour was never exhausted nor did the jar of oil become empty! Jezebel, a Queen, went down to her death fighting God. Her body was left to the dogs! (See 2 Kings 9:7,30-37). The widow of Zarephath, though in abject poverty, believed in God and lived!

There is an old New England saying:

*If you want to know what God thinks of money,
look at the people He gives it to.*

When we remember that Christ gave His life so that we
might have eternal life, it should be a joy to each of us to
return to Him *first* each week a portion of that which He
has entrusted to us.

In my experience I have met quite a few Christians who could be considered very wealthy. In every case I have found them unhappy and not committing their wealth to the cause of Christ. They have heaped luxury upon luxury upon themselves and forgot their first love. Now, I realize also that there are wealthy Christians who have "dedicated dollars" and for this I thank God.

It is better to have your bank in heaven than to have your heaven in a bank. In speaking around the country I am often asked what investment is best for a Christian to place his money...stocks, bonds, etc. I reply, the best place for a Christian to place his money is in a ministry of winning souls to Christ.

In this day of rising inflation, it is becoming increasingly difficult for a family to make ends meet. The average wage earner takes home 6 per cent more money each week this year than last year...but, because of inflation, his money is buying nearly 5 per cent *less!* The issuance of government food stamps have zoomed from an initial one billion dollars in 1968 to a present six billion dollars!

The first rule...and a rule that cannot be altered...that a Christian must learn if he expects his family to make ends meet is this:

From your salary each week...PAY GOD FIRST!

And give God at least one-tenth of your income. Thus, if your income is $150...give God $15 at least. What does God promise if you honour Him? Malachi 3:10-11 says that in such obedience:

1. Your Bible-believing Church will be able to carry out its ministry.
2. God will open the windows of Heaven and pour out His blessing on you and meet every need in your life and that of your family.
3. Your means of income will be preserved.

Take this first step and watch God work in your life!

Abraham bids Hagar leave, as Sarah watches.

Hagar was an Egyptian handmaid to Sarah, wife of Abraham. According to the law of those days a bondslave, like Hagar, could claim emancipation after six years service (Deuteronomy 15:12,17). If the slave belonged to her master's wife, she could not become the concubine of her master without the wife's consent (Genesis 16:12; 30:3,9).

Sarah was Abraham's half-sister. In ancient times marriage to half-sisters was not uncommon. When Abraham left his home town of Ur, Sarah was about 65. When she reached the age of 75 she was still childless. She was aware that God had promised Abraham that a child "shall come forth from your own body" (Genesis 15:4) and that the seed from this union shall be as numerous as the stars in heaven (Genesis 15:5).

But Sarah was old and she believed she could not become pregnant so she tried to help God. She convinced Abraham to let her handmaid, Hagar, become his concubine. In Bible days a concubine was a woman lawfully united in marriage to a man but in a relation inferior to that of the regular wife. Such concubines enjoyed no rights, but the right of lawful cohabitation. They had no authority in the family or in the household affairs. Their children, however, were considered as legitimate.

Sarah said to Abraham:

> *Please go in to my maid; perhaps I shall obtain children through her...And he went in to Hagar, and she conceived; and when she saw that she had conceived, her mistress was despised in her sight.*
>
> *(Genesis 16:2,4)*

Hagar, forgetting her position, proud of her pregnancy, despised the childless Sarah. Sarah became overbearing. Her plan was not working smoothly. She blamed her husband (Genesis 16:5) for Hagar's pregnancy and her attitude. Sarah called on the Lord for judgment. Abraham, knowing better than to get into a fight with two women, refused to interfere. He renounced his rights over Hagar and put her entirely at Sarah's disposal. Sarah undoubtedly nagged at Hagar, and the Scriptures tell us she treated Hagar harshly. The situation became so intolerable that Hagar ran away. She could not any longer take the nagging, in this case, however, from another woman! Hagar soon returned and bore Abraham a son. His name was Ishmael. And to this day there is enmity between Jew and Arab!

A *wife should be as refreshing to her husband as the dew-drops are to the rose...gentle as the rain yet shimmering in an inward beauty that transcends life's circumstances.*

An overbearing wife makes it impossible for a man to sit, stand, work or sleep without her continual and perpetual nagging.

> *A continual dropping in a very rainy day and a contentious woman are alike;*
>
> *Whosoever hideth her hideth the wind, and the ointment of his right hand betrayeth him.*
>
> (Proverbs 27:15,16)

A contentious woman...one who is nagging and always ready for a fight...can no more be stopped than the wind. Like the aromatic oil or perfume on your hands...as the perfume is impossible to hide...so is the nagging wife!

One day, when a grocer complained about Mrs. Lincoln's burst of temper, Mr. Lincoln laid a hand on the grocer's shoulder and murmered: "Can you not stand for fifteen minutes what I have stood for fifteen years?"

There are some 50 diseases which are caused by emotional stress. An overbearing wife can send her husband to an early grave.

In many cases a wife is overbearing because of real or imagined problems caused by her husband. As a husband, write on a sheet of paper those particular things that trigger your wife into becoming overbearing. Are you sloppy, careless, spend your money unwisely? Are you inconsiderate? Are you, yourself overbearing? If you are the cause of her attitude, then unless you correct your selfish habits...you are sinning against God. As a husband, it is true that you are the head of the house—but your wife is the neck that turns the head!

As a Christian wife, your outward testimony is a reflection of your inward life. If you are overbearing it is a sure indication that you are an immature Christian. As a wife you are reminded in 1 Peter 3:1-6 to be submissive to your husband. To help calm your nerves, go to your health food store and buy a B-complex stress supplement. And when you find yourself about to nag...instead, pray, asking God's grace.

Pilate, not heeding his wife's advice, washed his hands of the entire proceedings.

Only 38 words appear in the Bible about Pilate's wife. Yet she goes down in history as a woman of strong conviction who knew right from wrong.

Pontius Pilate was sent from Rome to become the 5th procurator of Palestine. Under his authority he possessed civil, military and criminal jurisdiction. His job was to govern the Jews who had often proven troublesome to Rome.

Pilate seemed to take pleasure in creating conflict among the Jews. One time he brought into Jerusalem under cover of night a group of soldiers carrying standards that bore the insignia of the Emperor of Rome. He knew this would inflame the Jews and it did. For five days Jewish leaders tried to gain an audience with Pilate to protest. He refused to hear them. On the sixth day he took his place on the judgment seat. When the Jews were admitted he had them surrounded with soldiers. He then threatened them with instant death unless they left and stopped troubling him.

The Jews surprised him. Each of them lay down on the ground...made bare their necks, declaring they preferred death rather than seeing their laws violated. Pilate had to back down. He could not slay so many Jews on such grounds without starting a civil rebellion. Reluctantly he ordered the poles bearing the Emperor's standards removed.

Pilate's wife undoubtedly heard many similar stories of her husband's overbearing personality. In the Herodian palace in which she lived she could at times look out and see multitudes following a man named Jesus. And it becomes apparent that she had compassion on him. The mob demanded the death of Jesus. Pilate's wife had a dream, however, while Pilate was deciding what to do with Jesus. His wife sent a servant to tell Pilate of her dream...imploring Pilate not to condemn Jesus. But though she was Pilate's wife, she could not overcome his stubborn and fearful personality. She tried to temper Pilate's violence but she failed.

Her dream of warning came true. Pilate's administration ended abruptly and he was banished from Palestine and ultimately, it is believed, committed suicide.

ADVICE TO HUSBANDS

If you'd lead a happy life
Never argue with your wife,
Often call her "Dear" and "Honey"
Always give her all the money,
Often praise her bonnet new,
Let her run your business too;
Say the cooking was divine,
That the socks were mended fine,
And that angels in the skies
Never had such hair and eyes;
Stay right in the house each night,
Say her mother was all right;
Meekly creep around the house
Like some helpless little mouse—
And if this wisdom you should doubt,
Disobey, and you'll find out.

One irate husband was once heard to remark to his wife:

> *Light bill, water bill, gas bill, milk bill — you've got to quit this wild spending!*

Husbands are of three types: prizes, consolation prizes and surprises. A husband is a man who expects his wife to be perfect and to understand why he isn't.

Most husbands who claim that they are henpecked might try increasing their wives' chicken feed allowances.

When a man and woman marry, they become one. Of course, they must decide *which* one, and that is often where the storm starts.

Seriously a husband and wife should combine their best qualities as one and recognize their faults. Too often a husband fails to exercise humility. Humility leads to strength and not to weakness.

Are you the type of husband that believes you are God's answer to perfection...that you are king and your wife is the dust of the earth? If so remember this, a king's reign is short but the dust will stay with us!

Learn to appreciate your wife. You take too much for granted. If your wife cooks the meals, does the housework, gives birth to your children, and then takes care of them... she works far harder than you...and without pay. If occasionally she becomes upset, irrational or unreasonable... remember so would you if you had her job.

Learn to be aware that she is there. Thank her for a wonderful dinner. Don't let a day go by without in some way you saying to her "I love you darling." It might be by a tender kiss, a compliment on her dress or cooking or a reassuring pat. Probably the greatest fault of Christian men today toward their wives is NEGLECT...a sure key to cause marital unhappiness.

Don't take her for granted! And don't think too highly of yourself. Women are the stronger sex. After all, where would you be without them?

Through his bitter marital experience, Hosea learned the
meaning of enduring and sorrowing love and forgiveness.
He experienced what God had gone through with Israel
forsaking Him. Then just as God took back Israel in forgiveness, Hosea was told to forgive and take back his stray-
ing wife.

The Northern Kingdom of Israel was enjoying prosperity.
And in prosperity, they sinned:

> There is swearing, deception, murder, stealing
> and adultery...Harlotry, wine, and new wine take
> away the understanding. My people consult their
> wooden idol...your daughters play the harlot, And
> your brides commit adultery.
>
> (Hosea 4:2,11,12,13)

This was a picture of Israel about 800 B.C. Yet is it not
also a picture also of today?

Yet God, in His infinite wisdom, commanded Hosea "Go,
take to yourself a wife of harlotry, and have children of
harlotry...So he went and took Gomer the daughter of
Diblaim, and she conceived and bore him a son" (Hosea
1:2-3).

Gomer, apparently was a sexually attractive young woman
...a product of her day. Her name, it is believed, meant
"destruction by idolatry." It is quite possible she would be
like many nominal religious people of today...without any
spiritual depth. But, nevertheless, Hosea obeyed God.
Gomer conceived and bore Hosea a son, Jezreel, and soon
she had two more children.

But Gomer soon slipped back into her role as a prostitute.
God used this to illustrate His own plight with Israel, to
whom He appealed,

> ...let her put away her harlotry from her face,
> And her adultery from between her breasts,
> Lest I strip her naked
> And expose her as on the day when she was born.
>
> (Hosea 2:2-3)

Nevertheless Hosea continued to love Gomer, even after
she left him. "For she said, I will go after my lovers, Who
give me my bread and my water, My wool and my flax, my
oil and my drink" (Hosea 2:5). Hosea found her, perhaps
in the slave market, and bought her back for about $2 and
eight bushels of barley (Hosea 3:2). It was like a second
honeymoon.

Perhaps no marriage would seem as impossible as a man marrying a known prostitute. Such a marriage would be filled with problems. Yet Hosea proved faithful not only to the Lord but also to his erring wife.

True, he was righteously indignant at her for her sexual permissiveness. Yet, in spite of her indiscretions, when she finally was down and out, he redeemed her from the slave market and actually courted her as he would court his first sweetheart.

A mate may have many faults...yet perhaps the hardest fault to forgive is when one mate shares that love with someone *other* than the person to whom he or she is married. This physical sharing of one's love becomes such a shocking sin that it takes a great deal of grace to forgive. And yet God directs us to not only forgive but also to remain with that mate if there is a spirit of remorse for the sin committed.

Paul in 1 Corinthians 7:12-15 gives us this wise advice:

> *...if any brother has a wife who is an unbeliever, and she consents to live with him, let him not send her away. And a woman who has an unbelieving husband, and he consents to live with her, let her not send her husband away.*

> *For the unbelieving husband is sanctified through his wife, and the unbelieving wife is sanctified through her believing husband; for otherwise your children are unclean [unblessed heathen, outside the Christian covenant], but now they are holy.*

> *Yet if the believing one leaves, let him leave; in such cases the remaining brother or sister is not morally bound...for God intended that we live together in peace.*

The last thing your mate wants to hear is you constantly nagging and pointing out the sin of the past. Once it is settled and forgiven...showing Scripturally that it is wrong, do not nag daily upon it. But then, pray asking God to come into your home and bring the sinner back to the Saviour. Your mate also is going through a terrible trial...filled with conflict. Pray through that conflict with love and with patient understanding.

While a Christian may sue out a divorce if the other party has been unfaithful (Matt. 19:9), such a procedure is not commanded—and in Hosea's case (when stoning was the penalty) forgiveness (grace) triumphed over law.

Your house can be a dream house but if there is friction within it will not be a home. Let your life be a beacon light that will guide your mate safely into God's harbour of eternal life.

Typical food market near Tel Aviv, Israel. In the days of Moses the Israelites longed to go back to Egypt for their leeks and garlic.

In an article on page 27 of the October, 1974 issue of *The Saturday Evening Post*, Dr. Linus Pauling, Nobel Prize winner, suggests: *"...the combined incidence of all diseases, at a given age, can be reduced one-half by the regular ingestion of between one and five grams of vitamin C per day."* He further suggests that following this daily routine could possibly increase one's life expectancy by eight years!

Moses had delivered his people out of Egypt. They had been personal witnesses to God's keeping power. They, however, had become so accustomed to blessings that they had gotten fat...not physically fat but spiritually lean!

In Deuteronomy 27-33 Moses gives the Israelites his third "Fireside Chat." Moses was about 120 years old. He first told his people what blessings they could enjoy if they would be obedient. He then told them what the results would be of their disobedience. They then in the years which followed chose the path of disobedience and were to be scattered (Deuteronomy 28:64). There would be no rest for them in the countries in which they resided (verse 65) and their life would be full of sorrow (verses 66-67).

> But Israel grew fat...you grew thick, you were gorged...you forsook God and began to follow foreign gods.
> (Deuteronomy 32:15-16)

We read in Nehemiah 8:1

> ...all the people gathered themselves together as one man into the street that was before the water gate; and they spoke unto Ezra, the scribe to bring the book of the law of Moses, which the Lord had commanded to Israel.

Ezra reminded them that, in the days of Moses the people of Israel

> ...took strong cities and a fat land, and possessed houses full of all goods...and fruit trees in abundance; so they did eat, and were filled, and became fat...

In the years 1972-74 the United States possessed abundance and fat and out of this self-sufficiency came the cancer of Watergate.

What we are reminded here is that, spiritually speaking, a nation or a people who allow themselves to become fat are in danger of slipping into sin and forgetting their heritage. Such an analogy could well be applied to those who overeat, gorging themselves to the point where they worship food.

In the race of life, your 100-**year** dash may end sooner than
you anticipated. It takes a lean horse for a long race.

A very stout man was walking on the boardwalk of a seaside town when he noticed a weighing machine with the notice: "I speak your weight."

He put a penny in the slot and stood on the platform. A voice answered: "One at a time, please!"

Remember those high school reunions where you discovered your one time flame not only kept her girlish figure ...but doubled it!

Obesity...fatness...is seldom caused by upset gland function. It can usually be traced to the intake of more food than is needed by the body.

It has been found that overweight people tend to have a shorter life-span. With obesity, the risk is greater for diabetes, high blood pressure, heart failure, gallbladder disease, varicose veins and hernia. Headaches, lassitude, irritability are seen more frequently in fat people. For some reason, unknown to doctors, cancer develops more often in fat people than in thin people.

With the food processing revolution we polished our rice, degerminated our flours and increased our intake of sugar. In just 11 generations our consumption of sugar has risen from 4 pounds of sugar a year to a record high of 175 pounds of sugar annually per person! Sugar makes us fat! Sugar causes a Vitamin B deficit and also causes metabolic disturbances.

Stress, anxiety and emotional tension tend to make carbohydrate-sensitive people fat, reports Dr. Robert C. Atkins.

If you find you are a compulsive eater because of problems in your life then pray asking God to meet your need. Leave your problems with Christ. Don't carry them around with you. Avoid fast reducing fads. Reduce your daily intake of carbohydrates (See your doctor for specific advice). Stay off of sugary desserts. Reduce your intake of bread. Check your spiritual temperature. Obesity is not always a sign of happiness.

Martha was so concerned about the temporal things of life that her time for spiritual matters was diminished.

Two sisters lived in a quiet little village on the southeast of the Mount of Olives, beside the Jericho Road. The town was Bethany. The two sisters, Mary and Martha.

Although they were sisters they had two quite different personalities. Mary, it seems, had never married. She was compassionate and imaginative. She did not allow ordinary household chores to control her life.

Martha, on the other hand, was the homemaker. She strove for perfection around the house. When Jesus came to visit them, Mary immediately sat at His feet in worshipful adoration. But Martha, like a buzzing bee, was more concerned with household details than with a quiet moment of courteous devotion. In Luke 10:40 we read:

> ...Martha was distracted with all her preparations; and she came up to Him, and said, "Lord, do You not care that my sister has left me to do all the serving alone? Then tell her to help me."

The Lord answered:

> ...Martha, Martha, you are worried and bothered about so many things; but only a few things are necessary, really only one; for Mary has chosen the good part, which shall not be taken away from her.   *(Luke 10:41-42)*

Both Mary and Martha witnessed Jesus raise their brother Lazarus from the dead. And six days before the Passover... the last feast attended by Jesus at Bethany...Martha again was probably busy in the kitchen. But it was Mary, because of her deep abiding love for her Saviour, who took a pound of very costly perfume valued at about $60 in those days ($250 today) and poured it on the feet of Jesus.

There are many Marthas today who strive for earthly perfection, sometimes at the cost of spiritual leanness. They allow little things in life...moles...to become mountains. Their life is one of constant nervous energy...busy doing everything. If you are a Martha, stewing over everything, try to calm down and keep in mind the Lord's words from Luke 10 above. Be sure that you choose "the good part" that will never be taken away from you.

Most everyone at one time or another suffers from nervous tension. Perhaps that is why Americans take 10 tons of aspirin daily. We are living in a very complex world. We have become slaves to our watches. Many of us try to keep up with the Jones'. Even the very thought of trying to make ends meet drives us up a proverbial wall. The credit card system has made it easier for people to buy the things they want *now* but it also has placed them in what seems to be eternal bondage to the credit companies!

Financial problems, marital problems, health problems... and even the absence of problems...winds up our nervous system and soon we find ourselves seeking release through an avalanche of tranquilizers. The United States can be said to be the most nervous and the most tranquilized population in the world!

What contributes to this nervous tension? Lack of proper nutrition is one major factor. Dr. Carlton Fredericks, on page 43 of his book, NUTRITION, *Your Key to Good Health,* states that in non-technical language: "...the central nervous system must 'breathe' to carry on. In its breathing processes, starches and sugars are burned up (oxidized). To burn these starches and sugars, certain chemicals are needed by the body. Among these necessary chemicals are several which the body cannot make for itself. These are vitamins, which should be provided by the diet."

The above is stated in more technical language, of course, in many nutrition and medical journals.

Vitamins are provided by one's diet. In this era of no-food foods and over-sugared foods and fast-food chains...a proper balance is not always achieved. When this occurs, the burning of the starches and sugars is interrupted and the normal activity of the nervous system is side-tracked.

I, personally, find that yogurt does wonders to calm a nervous stomach. I cannot stand plain yogurt but find the fruit flavored varieties easy to take. Doctors commend yogurt for its beneficial effects on the lower digestive tract.

When the nervous system has been abused...either by excessive worry or by a sugary/starchy diet lacking vitamins...it lets us know by creating a symptom we know as "nervousness." We become easily upset, disturbed by trivial things, sensitive to noise, easily offended and subject to worry a great deal. Anxiety is a key symptom.

The central nervous system may be protesting that your diet lacks enough of some of the B vitamins. Eating anything with sugar, such as fruits, cakes, ice cream simply compounds the problem. Dizziness, headaches and restlessness become commonplace. Many nutritional medical men recommend when B vitamins are used they should be used together...rather than simply taking B1 or B6. Many doctors agree that with today's eating habits, a daily vitamin supplement is advisable.

Then too, when worry and anxiety get you all wrought up, remember Peter's admonition "Casting all your care upon Him [God]; for He careth for you" (1 Peter 5:7). Ask for His forgiveness where you have sinned, make things right with your loved ones and friends, and then in prayer "cast all your care upon Him" and feel the burden lighten as you trust God to work things out according to His will.

My wife Mary and I have learned not to let the pressures of the day control us. Often, over the years, we have taken time off to go bicycle riding or walking. That which we cannot accomplish today...we know will be waiting for us tomorrow. Love and concern for others are the priorities that we want for our life. What about your life?

Job's friends were quick to give advice — the wrong advice!

Job had problems!

He finds himself stripped of family, friends, wealth and health and for no apparent reason.

His friends are of little help to him. In fact for seven long days and nights they sit with him in silence. Job had been a man whose life had purpose...but now he finds his life seemingly suddenly without either purpose or hope. He thus asks the question that many ask...why do the righteous suffer?

> *My soul is weary of my life...*
> *Is it right for Thee indeed to oppress,*
> *To reject the labor of Thy hands,*
> *And to look favorably on the schemes of the wicked?*
>
> *According to thy knowledge, I am indeed not guilty;*
> *Yet there is no deliverance from Thy hand.*
>
> *Thy hands fashioned and made me altogether,*
> *And wouldst Thou destroy me?*
>
> *(Job 10:1,3,7,8)*

Job's wife told him to "...Curse God, and die" (Job 2:9). In her voice of despair she was really saying that Job's religion was a failure. Job's friends suggested that Job had sinned and this was the cause of his problems. In the end Job lost his friends.

God had a purpose for Job's life that Job, within the confines of mere earth, could not understand. God, in a series of some 60 questions to Job, reveals Himself. And in this revelation Job admits: "I know that Thou canst do all things, And that no purpose of Thine can be thwarted...And I repent in dust and ashes" (Job 42:2,6).

In recognizing God, Job's purpose in life was restored. God returned his fortunes, more than he had before his trials. His riches included 14,000 sheep, 6000 camels, 1000 oxen and 1000 donkeys. And he lived another 140 years! Is it no wonder Job exclaimed even in the midst of his trial: "...He knoweth the way that I take; when He hath tested me, I shall come forth as gold" (Job 23:10).

Some people are like the fluffy seeds of the dandelion, which when blown, float lazily with no particular destination. The Apostle Paul tells us to *"Set your mind on the things above, not on the things that are on earth...and whatever you do in word or deed, do all in the name of the Lord Jesus..."(Colossians 3:2,17).* Encourage your children at an early age to seek Him daily for guidance and purpose in life.

Dr. Bob Jones, Sr. once said:

> It is better to die for something
> than to live for nothing.

Adlai Stevenson once questioned:

> With the supermarket as our temple and the sing-
> ing commercial as our litany, are we likely to fire
> the world with an irresistible vision of America's
> exalted purposes and inspiring way of life?

In today's fast-moving world where even a college education is no more a guarantee that one will get a job...it becomes difficult for a young person to find real purpose in life.

Many adults, as well, saddled by rising prices, find all they can do is merely exist. Television, with its "get-rich-quick" giveaway programs, its emphasis on violence and crime has been a major factor in creating a mood of dissatisfaction and uncertainty.

Many remember the well-known song sung so well by the late Mario Lanza:

> Ah! Sweet mystery of Life
> At Last, I've found you!

And ends with

> 'Tis love and love alone the world is seeking
> 'Tis the answer...'Tis the end of all of living!

This world's love, however, will not give your life direction nor purpose. Nor will it be the end of all of living. Life is not a cup to be drained, but a measure to be filled. For your life to have true desire and fulfilling purpose you must ask God to guide you:

> For thou art my rock and my fortress; therefore,
> for thy name's sake lead me, and guide me.
>
> *(Psalm 31:3)*

Dedicate your life wholly to God and God will provide a living desire in your heart filled with the purpose of serving Him.

Sodom and Gomorrah, cities singular for their evil and for the depravity of their inhabitants, were destroyed when the Lord rained fire and brimstone on them. See Genesis 19:24-25. Sodom is mentioned 36 times in the Bible. The destruction of the city, the wickedness of its citizens, and its willful disregard of God are often cited as an example or warning to others. See Deuteronomy 29:23, Isaiah 1:9-10, Jeremiah 23:14, 49:18, 50:40, Amos 4:11 and Matthew 10:15.

Prostitution and other forms of immorality, in many cities, were condoned. Many followed the pattern set by Roman emperors, living a life of homosexual sin and in some cases, one of bisexual advances.

During Paul and Timothy's day...sin ran rampant. The sins of homosexuality and lesbianism were just as prevalent then as they are today.

A woman of fashion might occupy several slaves for hours in just manicuring her nails and dressing her hair. Rich women bathed in milk. Jewelry was an important part of a woman's equipment. Will Durant writes that "Lollia Paulina once wore a dress covered from head to foot with emeralds and pearls that cost some one and a half million dollars!"

Lucius Aurelius Commodus, Roman Emperor from 161-192 A.D., tired of nothing to do, drank, gambled and wasted public funds. He kept a harem of 300 women and 300 boys. He forced some women devotees of the fertility goddess, Isis, to beat their breasts with pine cones till they died.

There are many references to illicit sex relations in both the New Testament and in the Old. Paul reminds the Corinthians in 1 Corinthians 6:9: "...do you not know that the unrighteous shall not inherit the kingdom of God?... neither fornicators, nor idolators, nor adulterers, nor effeminate, nor homosexuals."

Paul, in his letter to the Romans, shows that these of the ancient pagan world profess to be wise yet behave as fools (Romans 1:22). As in all sin, the sinner "...exchanged the truth of God for a lie, and worshiped and served the creature [the things made] rather than the Creator..." (Romans 1:25).

> For this reason God gave them over to degrading passions; for their women exchanged the natural function for that which is unnatural,
>
> and in the same way also the men abandoned the natural function of the woman and burned in their desire towards one another, men with men committing indecent acts and receiving in their own persons the due penalty of their error.
>
> (Romans 1:26-27)

God condemns such to everlasting punishment in Hell.

The theme of some soft drinks today is: LIVE. And some beer companies urge you to indulge in their product because "YOU ONLY GO AROUND ONCE!" This was the theme of those living during Paul's day in Rome and Greece.

Everybody today is fighting for their rights. Very few are taking time to fulfill their responsibilities.

The Gay Liberationists and the Lesbians (female homosexuals), parade unashamedly down big city streets fighting for the right to be recognized in today's society. They have even started their own churches.

And today's society does recognize them. Just as the drug culture is taking on an acceptance in today's world...so is immorality. Magazines available on public newsstands promoting such illicit relationships leave nothing for the imagination...they are very explicit both in photographs and words.

I have had people write me who were encircled in the sin of homosexuality and Lesbianism. They acknowledge their sin yet try to justify it by saying they cannot live without it, then they extol the "clean" virtues of their partner.

But God says such actions are unnatural affections. For those who would exchange "the glory of the incorruptible God for an image in the form of corruptible men," God says He will give "...them over in the lusts of their hearts to impurity, that their bodies might be dishonored..." (Romans 1:23-24).

When one keeps opposing God's directives for sexual purity (as well as other sins), we are reminded by Paul:

> ...just as they did not see fit to acknowledge God any longer, God gave them over to a depraved mind, to do those things which are not proper...
>
> and, although they know the ordinance of God, that those who practice such things are worthy of death, they not only do the same, but also give hearty approval to those who practice them.
> *(Romans 1:28,32)*

If this is your sin, repent of it and ask Christ to save you. Then ask God to deliver you from it. Stay away from every evidence of this temptation. Do not haunt the places you used to frequent. Disassociate yourself from those who contribute to your sin. And seek medical as well as spiritual guidance.

And when they came to the multitude, a man came up to Him, falling on his knees before Him, and saying,

Lord, have mercy on my son; for he is an epileptic, and is very ill; for he often falls into the fire, and often into the water.

And I brought him to Your disciples, and they could not cure him.

And Jesus answered and said, "O unbelieving and perverted generation, how long shall I be with you? How long shall I put up with you? Bring him here to Me."

And Jesus rebuked him, and the demon came out of him, and the boy was cured at once.

Then the disciples came to Jesus privately and said, "Why could we not cast it out?"

And He said to them, "Because of the littleness of your faith; for truly I say to you, if you have faith as a mustard seed, you shall say to this mountain, 'Move from here to there,' and it shall move; and nothing shall be impossible to you." (Matthew 17:14-20)

During the time of Christ, disease ran rampant. There were no 20th century physicians to go to, no x-rays, no anesthesia, no corner drugstores and no Geritol.

The hot summers with their brilliant light and their all-pervading dust, caused a great deal of eye disease. Then there was one of the most dreaded of all diseases, leprosy, which slowly ate away the tissues, attacking the limbs as well as the face.

Physicians adopted many forms of treatment. Oil was one of the most frequently used medicines. Some Jewish physicians recommended bleeding "every thirty days up to the age of 40." Even in those days some countries set the amount of doctors' fees and imposed penalties upon surgeons who were careless in performing operations.

Below is a description of the necessary qualification for a surgeon (since anesthesia had not been invented):

> A surgeon ought to be young, or, at any rate, not very old...he should neither hurry the operation... nor cut less than necessary, but do everything just as if the other's screams made no impression upon him.

Job, who loved God, was stripped of all his possessions, his family and his health. He was inflicted with a terrible case of boils from head to foot. Job said his troubles were heavier than "the sand from a thousand seashores" (Job 6:3). Job was afflicted with problems that would make our problems seem small. Yet, in the end he praised God and perhaps the key verse to his victory is Job 23:10:

> ...He knows the way I take;
> When He has tried me, I shall come forth as gold.

When Christ's diciples saw a man blind from birth (John 9:1-3), they asked the Master: "...who sinned, this man, or his parents, that he should be born blind? Jesus answered: It was neither that this man sinned, nor his parents; but it was in order that the works of God might be displayed in Him."

My wife Mary with our granddaughter, Jessica. Although we face the world with a smile, quite naturally our hearts are burdened. Yet we know the joy of the Lord is our strength (Nehemiah 8:10).

"Many are the afflictions of the righteous, but the Lord delivereth him out of them all" (Psalm 34:19).

The Surgeon-General requires that every pack of cigarettes contain a warning that they are injurious to health...yet, in spite of this, the sale of cigarettes increases every year. Alcoholism is one of the nation's leading health problems and causes some 50% of auto fatalities...yet the sale of liquors increases. "Up" pills and "down" pills are taken like candy. Grown, intelligent men fight for the right to use marijuana. More and more chemical additives are put into our food. And we wonder why we are sick!

We are living in a day of great physical and mental stress. Many of today's illnesses have as their cause emotional upsets. Anxiety disrupts our body's functions.

Before we ask why do Christians suffer...we must keep in mind that Christ was the supreme sufferer. Jesus Christ was without sin, yet He willingly accepted suffering and death, so we might have Life!

Paul suffered. He had a thorn in the flesh, and he was also whipped 5 times and 3 times beaten with rods (2 Corinthians 11:24-28). Stephen was stoned to death. John the Baptist lost his head. Nearly everyone of the Apostles either were crucified or died a martyr's death.

Yet Paul had his eyes set on future glory...a time when he would be beyond earthly suffering when he said:

> we are afflicted in every way, but not crushed;
> perplexed, but not despairing;
> persecuted, but not forsaken;
> struck down, but not destroyed.   (2 Cor. 4:8-9)

Right now our son-in-law and daughter are going through deep waters. Their four month old baby, Jessica, was born with Hemangioma, a benign tumor of the blood vessels. It covers part of her face. Her right eye, swollen, has been closed almost since birth. We have taken her to blood specialists, x-ray specialists, eye specialists. We have been told healing is a slow, drawn-out process. As we look at Jessica we wish we could bear the illness for her. Yet we know God is real. We know God has a purpose. And we accept the fact that "...all things work together for good to them that love God" (Romans 8:28).

It was some 4000 years ago that one of the greatest love stories of the ages took place. Rebekah was observed by one of Abraham's servants at the local well at Nahor in Mesopotamia (now Iraq).

Eliezer, Abraham's servant, informed Rebekah of his mission...to find a wife for Isaac and then consulted with her mother and her brother, Laban. When asked if she would accept this marriage arrangement, Rebekah answered. "I will go" (Genesis 24:58).

Isaac, who was grieving the death of his mother, Sarah, saw Rebekah coming afar off. When the servant explained to Isaac how God had answered his father's prayer (Genesis 24:4):

> Isaac brought her into his mother Sarah's tent, and he took Rebekah, and she became his wife; and he loved her...
>
> *(Genesis 24:67)*

For some 20 years she had no children. When she finally gave birth it was to twins, Esau and Jacob. Esau at the age of 40 married a girl named Judith and also another girl named Basemath. Both were Hittite women. The Hittites were Canaanites and one of the three great powers which plagued early Israel.

Isaac was very upset with this marriage as was Rebekah. In fact the two Hittite women made life miserable for Isaac and Rebekah and they were bitter against Esau for marrying them. It caused great mental anguish. Esau later took two additional wives from his Uncle Ishmael's family.

Rebekah, angered by Esau's actions, and desirous of having her son Jacob become the leader of his people...planned a course of deception...deception that undoubtedly would cause her mental agony. She dressed Jacob in goat's skin so his father, Isaac would believe him to be Esau and give him the blessings that belong to the first-born son. The deception worked.

Jacob had to flee because of Esau's anger. Rebekah, in

mental anguish says: "I am tired of living because of the daughters of Heth; if Jacob takes a wife from the daughters of Heth, like these [Esau's wives], from the daughters of the land, what good will my life be to me?" (Genesis 27:46)

So Jacob was sent far away, to his Uncle Laban, to find a wife.

Rebekah would never see her son Jacob again and would spend her remaining years living with a son who would always remember his mother's part in deceiving him.

Jacob, by deception, received the blessing that belonged to the first-born son, Esau. From this day on Rebekah lived in mental anguish fearful of Esau's revenge.

When one for years aspires to become President of the United States and then makes it—that's success. But the fortunes of men and the whims of the people change as rapidly as the wind. And the man who was once hailed suddenly finds himself evicted from the highest office of the land...lonely, despondent, dejected. Mental depression sets in. The world shows little love or compassion. but "...the peace of God, which passeth all understanding, shall keep your hearts and minds through Christ Jesus" (Philippians 4:7).

Life in the 1920's, the 1930's and the 1940's was far simpler than life today. We are living in an upside down world whose values have completely changed. We look at some people who are bogged down by a problem in their life and we say to ourselves: "They should have our problem...then they would have something to worry about."

But their problem...as small as it may appear to you...is a giant stumbling block to them. A person emotionally exhausted by months of worry may gradually suffer from mental depression. A mother worried about the bad marriage of her daughter; a wife concerned about the infidelities of her husband; a mother who allows the poor scholastic standing of her son to become an obsession with her; a mother who is dismayed because her daughter is pregnant before marriage and "the entire church knows about it!"...all these and more, are common reasons for mental depression.

Depression is a body's expression of emotional exhaustion. Nothing makes you happy. If the sun is shining, you remark, "but tomorrow the weatherman predicts rain." If the Lord blesses you with life in the form of a baby, you remark "That poor child will have to face this awful world." If in the midst of a drought it rains, you say "Yes, but it can't last."

Mental depression and anxiety are a striking symptom, in some cases, of Vitamin B deficiencies. Check your eating habits. Are you eating an unbalanced diet, a great deal of sugary desserts, candy? Check with your doctor. I personally find a B supplement vitamin daily keeps me mentally healthy. It could do the same for you.

Unless there is a physical reason for your depression (and in most cases there is not), a mental depression comes through your own design and it is a sin against God. Christ tells us: "...do not be anxious for your life..." (Matthew 6:25). "Come to Me, all who are weary and heavy laden, and I will give you rest" (Matthew 11:28). And, most important: *casting all your anxiety upon Him,*

> *because He cares for you. (1 Peter 5:7)*

How did Paul answer discouragement?

> ...do not lose heart, but though our outer man is decaying, yet our inner man is being renewed day by day. For momentary, light affliction is producing for us an eternal weight of glory far beyond all comparison.
>
> (2 Corinthians 4:16-17)

"...Jews came from Antioch and Iconium, and having won over the multitudes, they stoned Paul [himself a Christian Jew] and dragged him out of the city, supposing him to be dead. but while the disciples stood around him, he arose and entered the city" (Acts 14:19-20).

Paul reminds us; "Five times I received from the Jews 39 lashes. Three times I was beaten with rods, once I was stoned, three times I was shipwrecked, a night and a day I have spent in the deep...I have been in labor and hardship through many sleepless nights, in hunger and thirst, often without food, in cold and exposure...[but this] ..momentary, light affliction is producing for us an eternal weight of glory far beyond all comparison" (2 Corinthians 11:24,25, 27; 4:17).

126

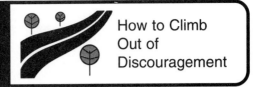
The apostle Paul had many problems!

Life was a great deal easier for him when he was a simple tentmaker in his hometown of Tarsus, a Roman city now in Turkey.

He was a Roman citizen and an excellent scholar. At about age 13 he went to Jerusalem to complete his studies under the famous Gamaliel (Acts 22:3). From there he became a persecutor of the Christians (Acts 8:1-4).

Then God met him on the road to Damascus and the persecutor became the persecuted. For in following Christ, he was to discover the trials and discouragement that such a decision brings with it. In 1 Corinthians 4:9-13 Paul relates:

> For, I think, God has exhibited us apostles last of all, as men condemned to death; because we have become a spectacle to the world, both to angels and to men.
>
> We are fools for Christ's sake...we are weak... we are without honor.
>
> To this present hour we are both hungry and thirsty, and poorly clothed, and are roughly treated, and are homeless:
>
> and we toil, working with our own hands,
> when we are reviled, we bless;
> when we are persecuted, we endure;
> when we are slandered, we try to conciliate;
> we have become as the scum of the world...

Yet this same Paul was to write 13 of the 27 books of the New Testament (14 if Hebrews was by him)...this man (who a second century writer described as) having a hooked nose, small stature, crooked legs and partly bald!

In the days before automobiles and airplanes he took three great missionary journeys, and a fourth journey to Rome, and travelled some 8500 miles! Paul was willing "...not only to be bound, but even to die...for the name of the Lord Jesus" (Acts 21:13).

Looking down our street in Huntingdon Valley you will notice a small green patch in the center of the road. Do you know what it is? It is a Sunburst Locust tree.

We have one in our front yard. A seed wafted into a small hole in the road...grasped firmly the scant dirt in the hole, rooted itself, and in the midst of every obstacle, emerged as a tiny tree! This photo shows how it looks when an adult views the scene...rather insignificant and unimportant. To us it does not appear as a problem.

But now look at this photo. I set the camera right on the road...level with the tree. And you can see how the problem suddenly is magnified and the miracle of the tree's very existence is realized.

Are not we as Christians like this tree, firmly planted in God's Word and to His promises, yet daily trampled by the traffic of the world and the darts of Satan? And yet, basking in God's sunshine of promises, in spite of all discouragements...we grow in grace!

Right now...as I write this page... I am discouraged... but not defeated! In fact, ever since I started writing this book I have been discouraged...but still not defeated.

More problems have arisen in these last weeks, while I have been writing this book, than perhaps in the entire last year. People think that just because I have been fortunate as an author, with my books selling well, that this would insulate me from problems.

Yet the livelihood of many people depends on my ability to write and to sell my books. And this brings with it an awesome responsibility. Right now bills from my printer total some $70,000. And right now my bank balance is about $2000. Now I am sure you can agree...that's a problem! And that can make one very discouraged!

But I know, without the shadow of a doubt, that God will answer this problem with a victorious solution. He always has. I always have been able in the past to meet my monthly printing bill...which is always my largest obligation.

We own no stocks nor bonds. Outside of $1000 in one bank, we have no savings account. And I know that there are many, many Christians whose problems are far, far greater than mine.

It's human to get discouraged. Can you imagine me sitting here in the heat of summer, flooded with problems, creating a book that is supposed to tell you HOW TO LIVE ABOVE AND BEYOND YOUR CIRCUMSTANCES? How can I give you advice? It's easy to explain. As I wrote this book...as I witnessed how Bible characters met and overcame problems...my own spiritual life...in this very writing ...became strengthened.

Now I praise God for many of the problems because although it is human to be discouraged, through Christ, we who lean on Him in trust can never...no never, be defeated!

So here, on this hot, humid day, I sit and type...while my son-in-law, Wes Frick, paints the basement below...and the fumes from the paint are about to overwhelm me. But I shall be steadfast and move on now to complete the next page of copy!

129

Solomon had it made!

He was the tenth son of David, and second by Bathsheba. Yet he became the third King of Israel, and reigned for 40 years!

One minute he was nothing. The next...King of Israel! Humbly he asked God to grant him one request:

> Give therefore thy servant an understanding heart to judge thy people, that I may discern between good and bad...
>
> *(1 Kings 3:9)*

And for a time he did have an understanding heart and could discern between good and evil. He was a great builder and a great organizer. He built the House of God, better known as "Solomon's Temple." This took seven years to build. The cost in today's money: approximately $174 BILLION!

But then he built his own gorgeous palace. And this took 13 years to build! We can only speculate on this a cost of about $80 BILLION! 1 Kings 7 gives an accurate description of all the costly materials that went into building.

But Solomon's life which started like a sun-filled day ended in torrential storms. He could not cope with success for success brought unlimited human power. Unfortunately he had two loves: The Lord (1 Kings 3:3) and many strange women (1 Kings 11:1). Solomon was a wise man. He wrote and collected some 3000 proverbs, 1005 songs. He is credited with writing the book Song of Solomon, the book of Proverbs and Ecclesiastes. He lost, however, his spiritual discernment for the sake of political advantage. And his love of women and voluptuous living brought his downfall. Solomon had 700 wives and 300 concubines (1 Kings 11:3)! Problems? Solomon had them! One thousand of them! He most likely never even met many of these women, having received them as gifts sealing political treaties. And many of them were idol worshippers. They encouraged him to worship other gods besides the Lord. So he worshipped

Ashtoreth, the goddess of the Sidonians, and Milcom, the horrible god of the Ammonites [where the image of the god sometimes was heated and the bodies of children who had just been slain were placed in its arms].

Solomon could not cope with success. Five steps led to his fall: [1] the ill-use of wealth (1 Kings 10:14-27); [2] the misuse of weapons (Deuteronomy 17:16; 1 Kings 10:26-29); [3] the lust for many women (1 Kings 11:1-3); [4] turning his heart away from God (1 Kings 11:4); and [5] outright idolatry (1 Kings 11:5).

Yes, Solomon had it made...but he could not cope with success!

Solomon conducts one of his hundreds of brides — an Egyptian princess — to her palace near the Temple. Solomon had a policy of cementing foreign alliances through numerous marriages to foreign noblewomen. When he married the daughter of Pharaoh she brought with her the town of Gezer as a dowry.

President Nixon devoted much of his entire life to gain the power of the Presidency. He had the ability in foreign affairs to be an outstanding President. Yet he could not cope with power. He could not cope with success. People, unfortunately, will not remember him as bringing the servicemen back from Vietnam. They will remember him for Watergate.

Very few people know how to cope with success.

I didn't!

In the early 1960's I was riding high, running a successful advertising agency. I had a million dollar account. The world was at my fingertips (but God wasn't)!

Suddenly I had nothing. God, in His mercy and wisdom, brought me to the lowest depths...turned me around and directed my path in His way! I learned the hard way.

Unfortunately, however, some people never learn how to cope with success. They feel because they are rich...because they have so called security and good health they have the world by the string. How foolish!

Some people think money is the answer to success. But very, very few Christians know how to handle money. Certainly any person who has not accepted Christ as personal Saviour cannot handle his money wisely!

Recently a man wrote a book titled THE LAZY MAN'S WAY TO RICHES. The book costs approximately 50¢ a copy to print. He sold it for $10 a copy! Within a short time he sold over 264,000 copies...at $10 a copy. That's $2,640,000. True, there were advertising costs to promote the book, but it is quite possible he cleared at least $1 MILLION. 264,000 people were willing to pay $10 in the hopes of becoming successful financially!

I know several millionaires. I've been on a first name basis with two of them...had many hours of fellowship with them ...dinners, etc. One is a born again Christian. The other knows what salvation is all about (his father was a minister) but he is following the teachings of a well-known cult. Both individuals are highly nervous. Both individuals are constantly striving to increase their wealth. In my own personal opinion, neither could cope with success.

Few people can cope with power. Give someone a position in the church...and quite often the power goes to his head. Perhaps your sincere prayer should be: "Lord, keep me poor and always in need...keep me from reaching the pinnacle of success. Keep me wholly leaning on Thee."

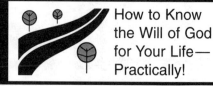
Gideon was a man of God. But his father, Joash, was an idolater. Sacrifices to Baal were common among his entire family.

Gideon was no doubt deeply troubled by this and believed that Israel's reverses were due to idol worship. An angel of the Lord appeared to Gideon and told him that he would be the instrument God would use to save Israel from the attacks of the Midianites...but he must first destroy his father's idols.

Gideon found it hard to believe that God could use one man to accomplish such a monumental task. So he asked God for a sign to make sure this action was the will of God for his life.

He hurried home, roasted a young goat, baked some unleavened bread. Then he took the meat and broth to the Angel who was beneath an oak tree. The Angel instructed him to place the meat and bread on a rock and then pour the broth over it. Then the angel of the Lord:

> ...put out the end of the staff that was in his hand
> and touched the meat and the unleavened bread;
> and fire sprang up from the rock and consumed
> the meat and unleavened bread...
>
> *(Judges 6:21)*

This was the first of four signs to Gideon to demonstrate the will of God (Judges 6:21,37-40; 7:9-15). So Gideon then went home and commanded ten servants to destroy the altar of Baal that his father worshipped.

Gideon and his army then proceeded to plan their war against the Midianites, making a preliminary encampment on the plain of Jezreel. Gideon then wanted another sign from God, "...If thou wilt save Israel by mine hand, as thou said..." (Judges 6:36).

Gideon placed some fleece [wool] on the threshing floor one evening. Then he told the Lord, "...If there is dew on the fleece only, and it is dry on all the ground, then I will know that Thou wilt deliver Israel through me, as Thou hast spoken" (Judges 6:37).

And God did just that! But Gideon still was not satisfied that this was the will of God. And he requested another test: "...let the fleece be dry and let the ground be wet" (Judges 6:39). God also fulfilled this request!

Gideon started out with an army of 32,000 men. God, aware that people would say that Gideon defeated the Midianites because he had a large army (rather than by God's hand) had Gideon pare down his army to just 300 men! The Midianites had an army of 135,000! Then by following God's will, Gideon soon was victorious (Judges 7:22)!

Gideon seeks God's will through a fleece.

Gideon needed a tangible sign, a fleece, because so very little of the Word of God had at that time been written. Also for a lone "no-body" to suddenly organize a revolt against an oppressing nation, there had to be an assurance that God was with him. But today, because we have the Bible, we do not need such tangible miracle signs. Many people today make the mistake of believing that some step in their life can only be taken if a fleece-type of demonstration is evidenced.

If you really want to know the will of God for your life... practically...then you must be willing to *follow* His will! Many people confuse His will with their own pre-determined will. An example: "I can't go to the mission field because we just got married and I'm going to have a baby; therefore we are seeking God's will for our life here in the United States." This is pre-determining God's will for your life by superimposing your will. God may allow you to stay in the United States as His <u>permissive</u> will but your life may never reach the rich fullness of blessing and fulfillment as if you had followed His <u>desired</u> will!

To know God's will for your life:

1. Determine to accept an unreserved commitment to His will.
   Present your body a "living sacrifice" (Romans 12:1).

2. See His will through the Word of God.
   "Thy Word is a lamp unto my feet, and a light unto my path" (Psalm 119:105). As J. Dwight Pentecost has so well put it: "God's will is revealed in His Word. God's will is God's Word, and God's Word is God's will."

3. Seek the guidance of the Holy Spirit.
   God's Word and the Holy Spirit work in harmony. If you take a step, believing it is of the Holy Spirit, and you are confused, ill at ease and restless...than it may not be of the Holy Spirit. The Holy Spirit does not exhibit Himself by confusion but rather by perfect peace of heart.

4. Consider circumstances.

   This beacon has to be used carefully, and sometimes one has to go against the circumstances! Nevertheless, God did give us brains to use, and to think things out sensibly is not unspiritual. Thus a person who has shown no aptitude for a certain line of work should be cautious before he feels *led* to plunge ahead into such a line.

5. Consult Christians.

   While there are stories of cases where a person felt led to go counter to the advise of experienced Christian friends, the Bible tells us that "...in the multitude of counselors, there is safety" (Proverbs 11:14).

Once you determine God's will...follow it. God's will does not change every 3 days or every month. When Gideon determined God's will...even though he had only 300 men... he charged against 135,000 and came forth victorious!

God's will on some matters is not something that is hidden that you must look for. On the things commanded by God's word, His will is clear. To be a homosexual is not God's will. It is in direct opposition to God's Word. To marry a non-Christian is not God's will. It, too, is in direct opposition to God's Word, etc.

On the decisions of life (Shall we move? Should I marry Roy? etc.), God is anxious to reveal His will for your life. But your spiritual life, your vessel, must be clean and dedicated, ready to accept His cup of blessing!

Seeking God's will is much like planting a garden. To plant a garden, you cultivate the soil, put the seeds in the ground, water and weed. Soon beautiful flowers appear giving off a sweet fragrance.

In seeking God's will, you plant your life in God's hands, cultivate His will through a garden of prayer, weeding out sin, and in so doing, keep your mind and heart open to His guidance. In due time you will blossom as a mature Christian fulfilling the will of God for your life.

The abundance of children is lauded in Psalm 128 which, in part, reads:

Your life shall be like a fruitful vine,
Within your house,
Your children like olive plants
Around your table.
Behold, for thus shall the man be blessed
Who fears the Lord...
Indeed, may you see your children's children.

And Psalm 127:3-5 reminds us: "Behold, children are a gift of the Lord; The fruit of the womb is a reward. Like arrows in the hand of a warrior, So are the children of one's youth. How blessed is the man whose quiver is full of them..."

God put a curse on the serpent, a curse upon the woman, and a curse upon man and the earth. For the woman, God said:

> *I will greatly multiply*
> *Your pain in childbirth,*
> *In pain you shall bring forth children;*
>
> *(Genesis 3:16)*

But God went on to further say in that same verse that in spite of the fact that you will realize that childbirth will give you pain; nevertheless, you will continue to welcome your husband's affections, and your husband shall become your master.

God's curse was not in having children (this was commanded before the Fall; see Genesis 1:26-28), but it was in allowing sorrow in the childbirth process. Incidentally, during the Millennium, there probably will be almost no pain in childbirth.

At least 15 times in Scripture the words "pain" and "travail" are used in reference to childbirth. Then too, in Bible days the process of giving birth was not as pain-free and sophisticated as it is in today's modern, well-equipped hospitals.

The women of Israel prided themselves upon having their babies quickly. They were helped, at times, by midwives; but in Mary's case, hers was born alone in a stable in Bethlehem. It was the duty of the mother to nurse the child, sometimes for as long as three years, in order to spare the child the diseases of the climate.

If the child were a son, the congratulations were many and warm. If the child were a daughter, they were less enthusiastic, in fact so less enthusiastic that sometimes they were more like expressions of sympathy. "Girls are but an illusory treasure," observed the Talmud; and then adds, "besides, they have to be watched continually."

Childbirth in Bible days brought much pain. There was no anesthesia, no pain-killing drugs and none of the conveniences that women enjoy today.

In the fall of 1973, our son-in-law, Wes Frick, enclosed our patio so we could use this area all year round. In this scene you see the bare wood frame prior to finishing, and our bird feeder through the open window. The element that brings joy to us is not the feeder, but the birds that will flock here for food, chirping and warbling.

And, likewise, the framed structure that we live in is a house. But it doesn't really become a home without the joy of children. The trials and inconveniences of building a home and the monthly mortgage payments are willing sacrifices we make for the ensueing happiness that comes from seeing our families grow up.

HOW TO FACE FEAR

Fear of Childbirth

In some measure, fear of childbirth exists because everyone has a fear of the unknown.

This is particularly true of the women who has never had the experience of childbirth. She may hear many "old-wives tales." And so-called good meaning friends, who have already had children, sometimes in a desire to raise their stature, exaggerate the agony and trials they went through.

The childbirth experiences of one person, however, are not necessarily duplicated in another. Each human body is different. Each childbirth is different.

Some of the fear of childbirth can be alleviated by purchasing a good book on the subject.

Certainly childbirth today is much safer and easier than in the Middle Ages when rusty forceps were used and sterilization of the surroundings was not practiced.

Those who have gone through childbirth will tell you that the brief time of discomfort in labor is suddenly all forgotten with the joy of giving birth! If this were not true, women would remember this pain...and would refuse to have further children.

Many describe labor as similar to a "severe case of cramps during menstruation but occurring in increasingly closer intervals." At times they may seem unbearable but at this point pain deadeners are given. Then, too, such pains become more bearable when one is prepared on how to relax the muscles to ease tension.

God promises:

> Women shall be preserved through the bearing of
> children if they continue in faith and love and
> sanctity with self restraint.
>
> (1 Timothy 2:15)

"They that sow in tears shall reap in joy" (Psalm 126:5). And the fleeting moments of trial in childbirth will be rewarded by the far greater joy of giving life to a son or daughter. Remember, "The Lord is my strength and song, and is become my salvation" (Psalm 118:14).

In the days of Moses, during the wilderness journey, the brazen serpent of brass brought healing to the Israelites. Whoever looked at it was healed. See Numbers 21:4-9. This brazen serpent was a type of our Lord bearing our sins on the cross (John 3:14-16). Today, the medical profession uses an emblem which pictures a coiled serpent. It is called a Caduceus.

One of Hammurabi's codes of law for surgeons around 1700 B.C. stated: *"If a physician performed a major operation on a free-man with a bronze lancet and has caused the free-man's death, or he opened up the eye socket of a free-man and has destroyed the free-man's eye, they shall cut off the physician's hand"* (Law section 218).

In Rome, shoemakers, barbers, carpenters...all practiced medicine. Cato, a Roman soldier and statesman (234-149 B.C.) stated that Greek physicians "seduce our wives, grow rich by feeding us poisons, learn by our suffering, and experiment by putting us to death."

About A.D. 100, military medicine in Rome reached its ancient zenith. Every legion had 24 surgeons. The profession reached a high degree of specialization during this age. There were urologists, gynecologists, obstetricians, ophthalmologists, dentists. There were even women doctors who wrote manuals on abortion.

Yet, in spite of all this, much superstition entered into treating the sick, and the various facets of medicine, though practiced, were not perfected as we know them today.

The Apostle himself experienced a lingering illness. He wrote,

> And lest I should be exalted above measure through the abundance of the revelations, there was given to me a thorn in the flesh, the messenger of Satan to buffet me, lest I should be exalted above measure.
>
> *(2 Corinthians 12:7)*

Whether this thorn was an eye ailment which caused Paul to have to write in his large sized letters, we are not certain. Perhaps this is why Luke the physician travelled with him. In any case, we do know that three times he prayed for deliverance from this thorn. But the Lord answered:

> My grace is sufficient for thee: for my strength is made perfect in weakness.
>
> *(2 Corinthians 12:9)*

Paul, who at times had to make missionary journeys traveling on foot through mountain passes some 10,000 feet high, perhaps in the snow, knew what trials were. He was about 65 at the time! Yet, in his ailments, without the medical and surgical skill of today, he learned to "...glory in my infirmities, that the power of Christ may rest upon me" (2 Corinthians 12:9).

Doctor:
Nixon Afraid
Says His Patient
Fears Hospital

Associated Press

NEW YORK — Air Force Maj. Gen. Walter Tkach said Saturday that he decided against hospitalizing Richard M. Nixon after the former President told him, "If I go into the hospital, I'll never come out alive."

Unfortunately many hospitals have been designed by people who must have taken their architectural training in the Dark Ages. They are void of warmth and their very atmosphere sets a patient on edge. And many personnel operate in the same cold, harsh manner. It's time for a change!

Someone has said that "doctors make the worst patients." When suddenly they find themselves waiting endlessly in a waiting room or pushing the buzzer for service only to find the nurse arriving an hour later...then they soon have empathy for the patient.

Medicine, until the third century, was largely a matter of family herbs, magic and prayer. However, there were slave doctors and quacks in Rome five centuries before Christ. The first freeman physician in Rome was Archagathus the Peloponnesian (the Greek). His mania for cutting and burning won him the name of Carnifex, butcher.

Medical doctors are not God. They are human. They do not have all the answers. There are wonderful and fine doctors and there are also some bad ones.

If a doctor suggests you have an operation it is wise to get two or three other medical opinions.

HOW TO FACE FEAR

Fear of an Operation

The American doctor operates a financially successful enterprise, one with no professional equal. His average gross income is close to $90,000 a year with a large percentage admitting an even higher income of $110,000. There are about 150 doctors in the U.S. to every 100,000 people. The modern doctor works about ten hours a day, although recent survey shows that 26% now work 48 hours or less a week.

Of 430,000 appendectomies performed each year, almost 100,000 are probably unneeded. A Los Angeles gynecologist investigated 6248 hysterectomy operations and found that 30% of the women aged twenty to twenty-nine had no disease whatsoever! In another survey, 56% of all gynecological procedures were judged to be either unnecessary or doubtful.

So it is important that prior to submitting to an operation you do have the counsel of more than one physician. And when that counsel is given it would be better to secure it from physicians who are unaware of the other's judgment.

There are times, however, when surgery is advisable and necessary. However, why not follow Scriptures and first:

> ...call for the elders of the church; and let them pray over him, anointing him with oil in the name of the Lord; And the prayer of faith shall save the sick, and the Lord shall raise him up; and if ye have committed sins, they shall be forgiven him.
> (James 5:14,15)

All illnesses are not healed by prayer. When surgery is indicated remember Psalm 34:7:

> The angel of the Lord encampeth round about those who fear him, and delivereth them.

What greater promise can be yours! Look to your hospitalization as a further opportunity to witness to your physician, to your nurses, to those around you, that Christ the Great Physician can heal them of their sins and give them eternal life!

David meeting Abishag, the Shunammite girl.

David had lived a full life. He conquered Goliath, he was made king over Judah and then all Israel. He was versatile; a shepherd boy, a court musician, soldier, outcast captain, king, loving father, poet, sinner. The late Henrietta C. Mears called him "the Robin Hood of the Bible." He reigned for forty years.

Humanly speaking, he was sexually active. And it was his sin with beautiful Bathsheba that caused tragedy in his own family. David had nine wives and many concubines. He left 10 concubines in Jerusalem when he fled from Absalom. He had 19 known sons from them.

David also from his nine wives had another 19 sons and many daughters of which Tamar was one.

But now David was approaching 70. The hardships and privations of his early years and the self-indulgence of his polygamous life in mature manhood had weakened him.

His natural heat was so wasted that no clothes could keep him warm. Absalom's rebellion had been the final blow that diminished any desire for living...Absalom, his own son!

> So his servants said to him, "Let them seek a young virgin for my lord the king, and let her attend the king and become his nurse; and let her lie in your bosom, that my lord the king may keep warm." (1 Kings 1:2)

This suggestion was an accepted medical prescription, according to historians, even down to the Middle Ages.

> So they searched for a beautiful girl throughout all the territory of Israel, and found Abishag the Shunammite, and brought her to the King.

> And the girl was very beautiful, and she became the king's nurse, and served him, but the king did not cohabit with her. (1 Kings 1:3)

David's triumphs and trials had left him physically incapable even of maintaining adequate body heat. And soon after that, he died.

Take an inventory of your life...honestly. This may cause you to discover what is causing your problem. Then seek to correct it.

Freedom from disturbing problems of life, good health...all contribute to satisfying marital relations.

David had many ups and downs in his life and only lived until 70...a young age to die in his day.

While Moses lived to be 120 and the Bible tells us:

> *Although Moses was one hundred and twenty years old when he died, his eye was not dim, nor his vigor abated.*
>
> *(Deuteronomy 34:7)*

Impotency is complete failure or serious impairment of sexual power and is more prevalent in the male.

Many doctors believe that there are more cases of impotency today than twenty or thirty years ago. Much of this is because of the new permissiveness of our society, increasing moral laxity, the rise of pornography and premarital relations. These increasing temptations, particularly on the male, affect a marriage and often cause impotence.

In an attempt to stimulate sexual potency, both men and women have dosed themselves with a variety of drugs and chemicals. There appears to be general agreement that impotency in the male (and frigidity in the female) originate more often with purely emotional disturbances rather than inadequacy of diet.

One doctor of nutrition suggests a stress vitamin supplement of B Complex and C. PABA (Para-Aminobenzoic Acid), part of the B Complex range is also suggested...as little as 100 mgs, a day, combined with a Vitamin E supplement. Since sexual function depends on the functions of the nerves, such supplements which promote the stability of the nervous system should be considered important to healthy sexual function. Naturally, consult your doctor.

It is important, first, that you take an inventory of your life. If you are cheating on your mate, if there is sin in your life, if you have not accepted Jesus Christ as your personal Saviour and Lord...then first, confess your sin, redirect your path and "...seek first His kingdom and His righteousness and all these thing shall be added to you" (Matthew 6:33). Remember, don't take your problems to bed. Leave them by prayer, in God's hands. He is able!

It is difficult to find specific illustrations of a Bible character who had a fear of growing old. There are indications, however, by the actions of some people in Scriptures, that they wanted to remain young.

Only 15 words tell the story of Lot's wife. Her name is not even mentioned. But one thing is certain...the story of Lot's wife is familiar today even to children.

And the second shortest verse in the Bible is found in Luke 17:32:

Remember Lot's wife.

Jesus had been speaking of the days of Lot when those of Sodom and her sister cities of the plain lived the luxurious life of the rich, eating, drinking, building...and all their activity ended in destruction.

The Scriptures give us the impression that Lot's wife lived for the things of the world. Her husband was moderately rich and influential (Genesis 13:10-11). Quite possibly she indulged in all the health spas of the day...and if plastic surgery were possible in that day, she most likely would have had her face lifted.

Lot was Abraham's nephew. Both Lot and Abraham were in Egypt when famine came. They returned to Bethel, where their flocks multiplied so rapidly that Abraham suggested they divide...one going to the East...one to the West. Lot, taking a long look at the fertile plains of the Jordan River, chose this area. He married a woman of Sodom (for the area he had chosen was the area of Sodom and Gomorrah).

So Lot pitched his tent in Sodom a city of homosexuals and sodomites (Genesis 19:5). One evening two angels came to Lot and told him "...we will destroy this place, because their outcry has become so great before the Lord that the Lord has sent us to destroy it" (Genesis 19:13). The next day they urged Lot and his family to leave...but they lingered, hesitating to leave the pleasures of sin. The angels finally forcibly removed them from the city and urged them to run.

All did run and they were told "...look not behind thee..." (Genesis 19:17). But Lot's wife, anxious to hold on to the pleasures of sin which perhaps she thought would give her a perpetual youth, looked back. And because she was not willing to press forward, but rather longed for the exhilerations of yesterday, she was turned into a pillar of salt —probably by the falling upon her of some of the divinely caused erupting burning sulfur and lava which was now burying the city in judgment (Genesis 19:26).

Lot's wife was afraid to move forward. To her life was in looking back. In reality, however, looking back brought her death. Facing the future triumphantly and obeying God would have brought her life!

My good friend and Bible scholar, Dr. Gary G. Cohen, reminded me that in ancient days old people were more honored than today. With old age came added wisdom, respect, and authority. And because of this...there was a built-in compensation in Bible days for growing old.

The same used to be true for centuries in China, where one's honor increased with his age. The modern communist Cultural Revolution of the 1960's largely reversed this, however, and in today's China many of the older people are no longer respected. How sad!

When Joseph brought his father, Jacob, before Pharaoh, the ruler asked Jacob:

> ...How old art thou?
>
> And Jacob said unto Pharaoh, The days of the years of my pilgrimage are an hundred and thirty years; few and unpleasant have the days of the years of my life been, nor have they attained the years that my fathers lived during the days of their sojourning.
>
> (Genesis 47:8-9)

Oliver Wendell Holmes said on Julia Ward Howe's 70th birthday: "To be seventy years young is sometimes far more cheerful and hopeful than to be forty years old." The longest period in a woman's life is the 10 years between the time she is 39 and 40!

Love has no boundaries. Our grandson Darrell kisses my step-father and takes him for a walk. The difference in age — 70 years!

We are bombarded today with creams and lotions from turtle oil to honey whose advertisers promise the use of such will make us youthful. Several cosmetic manufacturers use placenta (afterbirth from the lining of the uterus) as the main ingredient in their "eternal youth" compounds. They find the $1 worth of ingredients sell better if they package it attractively and sell it in a $100 jar!

I can remember coming up from the basement one day and my daughter Dawn was at the top of the steps giggling. From that vantage point she could notice that my hair was thinning and a slight bald spot was noticeable on the crown. And one day when buying a suit, I looked in a 3-way mirror. And sure enough, I was growing old!

But growing old is relative. Look at it this way...70,80, 100 years is an extremely short time compared to an eternity. When you were young...you wanted to be 16. When you were 16, you wanted to be 21 and married. Once you get married, you want children. And when your children get married, you want grandchildren. Certainly you don't want to be 16 all your life!

The best advice one can give is that you should accept the fact that everyone (except for an untimely death), including today's newborn child...will grow old. One does not grow old by living — only by losing interest in living. If, like Lot's wife, you keep gazing fondly at yesterday...in your old age, you will miss the blessings God has in store for you today and tomorrow, and eternally!

Rather, like the Biblical ancients, let your wisdom increase with your age. Try to be a cheerful, sensible counsellor—yet not pushy—to the less experienced more energetic youth. *Principles of wisdom* endure (however, *methods* often need changing and updating).

Also put a few worthwhile projects "on the back burner" of the range of your life, so that after the hot cereal of youth has been fully cooked, there are still some worthwhile biscuits (projects, goals, jobs) that can be slowly browned.

On the road to Damascus, God brought Saul to an abrupt halt in his life and for three days he was without sight. Then God's will was revealed for his life and he became the greatest missionary the world has seen.

If you are afraid of facing life, you are doubting God's power to save and keep you (Jude 24). This is sin. Perhaps, like Saul, who became Paul, you should spend 3 days with God in meditation and prayer. In feasting on His Word, God will provide the answer for your life!

It was perhaps summer, 28 A.D.

Jesus Christ called his twelve disciples to him to be ordained. At the commissioning service he told them exactly what would lie ahead for their lives. This was not to be a picnic. They were in the Lord's work and they should be made aware of what was ahead and face life without fear but with total reliance upon God.

Their message:

> Preach
> Heal the sick
> Raise the dead
> Cast out demons   *(Matthew 10:7-8)*

Their personal equipment:

> *They were not to acquire gold or silver or copper for their money belts. Nor were they to take a bag, or even two tunics or sandals. See Matthew 10:9-10.*

Their future:

> *They would go forth as sheep in the midst of wolves; therefore they should be shrewd as serpents and innocent as doves.*
>
> *Brother will deliver up brother to death, and a father his child; and children will rise up against parents. And you will be hated by all on account of My name (Matthew 10:21-22).*

Then Christ reminds them:

> *...do not fear those who kill the body, but are unable to kill the soul; but rather fear Him who is able to destroy both soul and body in hell.*
>
> *(Matthew 10:28)*

Though they will be opposed on every hand and though they will be facing a multitude of problems Christ assures them:

> *...the very hairs of your head are all numbered. Therefore do not fear.*
>
> *(Matthew 10:30-31)*

Most every night before retiring either I or my wife or children prepare a late evening snack. Sometimes we even eat by candlelight. Soon the trials and pressure of the day fades in the warmth of the kitchen fellowship. We forget about life's cares and in our evening prayers commit our life to Him. The world's greatest time-waster is taking your problems to bed with you. Tossing and turning over them will not resolve the problem...but will endanger your health!

Eliminate the negatives in your life. Don't use the word "can't" in your vocabulary. The Christian life is a positive life...not a negative one. The Christian life is one of joy... not sadness.

HOW TO FACE FEAR

Fear of
Facing Life

I am surprised at how many Christians have a fear of facing life. Many, who should be serving the Lord full time, are satisfied with His second best because they desire temporal security.

Their life has become one monotonous routine. And anything that would disturb that routine creates an emotional problem for them.

If yours is a fear of facing life perhaps it is because you are not aware of God's promises for your life. Or, if you are aware, you doubt that God is able to solve your problems.

Many people who have a fear of facing life often harbor such fears not only throughout the day, but also in the night. Very few of these ever get a good night's sleep. They are restless and their nights have many sleepless hours. They wake up more tired than when they went to bed.

I personally have found restful sleep by the following simple formula. I eat a very light snack before bedtime (one shredded wheat in milk). And take the following vitamin supplements:

> 100 milligrams B6
> 100 milligrams Pantothenic Acid
> 250 milligrams Magnesium Oxide
> 500 milligrams Calcium Lactate

Of course, before taking any supplements, check with your doctor.

Every physician will agree that proper, satisfying rest is an important step towards mental wholesomeness.

Christ reminds us: "Are not two sparrows sold for a cent? And yet not one of them will fall to the ground apart from your Father...Therefore do not fear; you are of more value than many sparrows" (Matthew 10:29,31).

God is aware of every problem you have or imagine you have. And He sees past the problem. Satan would have you face life with fear. Through God's grace, by placing your trust *completely* in Him, you can face life with triumphant joy.

157

King Hezekiah is warned of his approaching death by Isaiah. The King pleads for more time.

One of Hezekiah's first acts was to reopen the Temple which his father had closed and desecrated. He also destroyed the idolatrous altars.

Moses, so beset by the complaints of his people, longed for death (Numbers 11:15).

Elijah, running for his life, from an angry Jezebel, prayed:

> *It is enough! Now, O Lord, take away my life...*
>
> *(1 Kings 19:4)*

Here are two saints of God who actually would have welcomed death!

But for Hezekiah...he was afraid to die.

Hezekiah was king of Judah for 29 years from c. 724 to 695 B.C. He lived during the founding of Rome and the early Olympics in Greece. It was Hezekiah's father, Ahaz, who followed the abominable rites of the Moabites by burning children in the fire (2 Chronicles 28:3). At 25 Hezekiah took over his father's reign.

About 704 B.C. Hezekiah, in spite of Isaiah's strenuous warnings (both against opposition to Assyria and alliance with other powers) made an alliance with Egypt. Hezekiah had at this time witnessed to his immediate north the captivity of his ten sister tribes of Israel by Assyria. King Hezekiah pleaded for peace. The king of Assyria demanded a peace settlement of $1,500,000.

To gather this amount, Hezekiah used all the silver stored in the Temple and in the palace treasury. He even stripped off the gold from the Temple door. The king of Assyria was not satisfied and prepared to capture Jerusalem. God intervened and at night the angel of the Lord killed 185,000 Assyrian troops (2 Kings 19:35).

But Hezekiah became deathly sick. Isaiah told him to set his affairs in order for the Lord said he would die (2 Kings 20:1). Hezekiah, in grief, turned his face to the wall and pleaded with the Lord that he had walked in truth, with a perfect heart and did that which is good in His sight. His prayer was 30 words. Then he broke down and cried.

Then suddenly...through Isaiah, God answered: "...I have heard your prayer. I have seen your tears...And I will add fifteen years to your life..." (2 Kings 20:5-6).

For the Christian, death offers you the opportunity to meet life's greatest challenge and break through earth's gravitational forces to be united with the Lord. Without any spaceship...without any spacesuit...within a brief instant you (your *spirit*—the real you) become a Heavenly astronaut. You become the inheritor of a life far beyond any human description, free from pain, from nervous tension, from anxiety. And most likely your first words upon reaching the victory shore will be: "How could I ever have wanted to remain longer on earth!"

The fear of death is largely due to our natural fear of both harm (here extinction) and of the unknown. Many say that no one has died and then come back to tell us of his or her experience in this transition. If someone could...then, perhaps, the fear of death would be diminished. Yet, this is precisely what Jesus did (Revelation 1:18)!

No healthy minded person, even though a Christian, yearns for death. But a Christian should face death unafraid and with calm assurance.

What is the earliest point in your life you can remember? When you were 2, 3 or 4 years old? What happened before that moment of your remembrance? You personally don't know. You go to bed perhaps at 11 PM. You wake up at 7 AM. Do you remember what occurred during the time from 11-7?

Then what is death? For the Christian it is a graduation day. The body *only* dies at the time of physical death. This is caused by the soul and spirit leaving the body. The body returns to dust and the soul and the spirit of the righteous (those who have accepted Jesus Christ as Lord and Saviour) go to heaven to await the resurrection (2 Corinthians 5:8).

The soul and the spirit of the wicked (those who have *not* accepted Christ as Saviour) go to hades (literally in the Greek, the "not-seen" world) to await the resurrection and then are destined to the "Lake of Fire" at the final judgment (Revelation 20:11-15).

Death for the Christian does not mean he enters into a sleep. It means his marking time on earth is done and his graduation day is here...he will be present with the Lord.

> *We are confident, I say, and willing rather to be absent from the body, and to be PRESENT WITH THE LORD.*
>
> *(2 Corinthians 5:8)*

You certainly would not want to spend your entire lifetime as a child. There comes a time when you want to grow and meet life's challenges.

Sarah means princess. And Sarah was a princess in much of her bearing and in her character.

Sarah married Abraham. Actually, she was her husband's half-sister on the side of their father Terah. Such marriages were not uncommon in those days.

When Sarah and her husband started their wanderings, they both were in their mature years. Sarah was 65. Abraham was 75. They first went to Haran (in southern Turkey). But because of a terrible famine, they were forced to flee to Egypt. Abraham, however, had a problem—Sarah was still uncommonly attractive when she was in her late middle age. Abraham was afraid of what the Egyptians might do to get rid of Sarah's husband, so he advised Sarah:

> ...when the Egyptians see you, they will say, "This is his wife;" and they will kill me, but they will let you live.   (Genesis 12:12)

So he passed Sarah off as his sister. Years later, Abraham did the same thing at the court of Abimelech, King of Gerar (Genesis 20:1-18). In each case God intervened to save Abraham, and the pagan rulers rebuked him for deceiving them.

At 75, still childless, she induced her husband Abraham to take her handmaid, Hagar, as a concubine. Ishmael was born to Hagar and the Arab race began. But when Sarah was 90 God opened her womb and she gave birth to Isaac. Prior to this birth she had laughed exclaiming:

> Shall I indeed bear a child, when I am so old?
> (Genesis 18:13)

And the Lord said to Abraham: "Is anything too difficult for the Lord?" (Genesis 18:14). The Bible tells us that Abraham believed God and had great faith: "...without becoming weak in faith he contemplated his own body, now as good as dead since he was about 100 years old, and the deadness of Sarah's womb...yet he did not waver in unbelief" (Romans 4:19-20). About some 4000 years ago Sarah became the Mother of Nations.

Years passed. Then...quite possibly Abraham was some 24 miles away at Beersheba near part of his vast herds when he received notice that Sarah had died. Sarah was 127 years old. In fact Sarah is the only woman whose age at death is mentioned in the Scriptures!

Sarah died at Hebron. In the selection of the site for his wife's last resting place (the Cave of Machpelah), Abraham demonstrated his great affection for her. In Genesis 23:2 we are told that he mourned her. A few years later, Isaac on his wedding night, took his bride Rebekah, to what had been Sarah's tent, thus showing how fondly he, too, cherished his mother's memory.

Abraham passes Sarah off as his sister at the court of the Pharaoh. One sage quoted in the Talmud stated that Sarah was so beautiful that "...all other women looked like apes in comparison." Sarah died at the age of 127 and was buried in Hebron.

After living with someone for 15 or 20 years or more that person becomes actually an extension of yourself. Through physical and spiritual union your mate becomes a part of you.

And when that part of you goes on into eternity...something in you dies. Your mate was the spark that kept the fire in your heart burning. With that spark no longer there... soon the fire dies out.

It is a difficult time of transition. You see other married couples around you, your friends, still enjoying life, and you resent them. Why did God have to remove your loved one? Perhaps this is a more difficult time for a widow. When a man loses his wife he has his job to keep him occupied. But if a widow is a homemaker she may find herself withdrawing from society and becoming bitter.

My personal observation is that part of the problem lies with the church...particularly the church that is more interested in the numbers game of building up a big congregation than in a continual ministry to their faithful members. It is the responsibility of the church to support widows who have no relatives or have relatives unable to support them (1 Timothy 5:3,16). To my knowledge this admonition is not being followed faithfully by our churches! In most churches widows are not considered in programming fellowship groups. They no longer can share in the Married Couples Sunday School classes or fellowships without feeling awkward.

A Christless home goes to pieces when sorrow strikes. When, however, John the Baptist was beheaded you remember "...his disciples came, and took up the body, and buried it, and went and told Jesus" (Matthew 14:12). In a grave they buried John, and in the heart of Jesus they buried their sorrow. To have Jesus as our Saviour and Guide means that we have One well able to protect and console our hearts when the first shadow falls across the home. Because we belong to God, His loving heart is touched with our grief. In all our sorrows we have a Friend who experienced sorrows no others ever have. All our sorrow will be turned to joy. One day there will be no more anguish (John 16:20-21). "They that sow in tears shall reap in joy" (Psalm 126:5).

Your mate has gone on to Coronation Day and awaits you. For victory in your life, keep active in God's work. Do not withdraw yourself from society. For in so doing you question the precious promises of God and rob yourself of the precious joy of serving Him who suffered so you might have life...and have it abundantly!

"Is anything too difficult for the Lord" (Genesis 18:14)? NO! Go in the strength of the Lord God. For your strength will be made perfect in weakness (Psalm 71:16; 2 Corinthians 12:9-12).

I remember in the fall of 1968 watching the sunset in the Holy Land. This was my first trip and I enjoyed it immensely. Yet as much as I liked it, I remember thinking..."this same sun is now rising back home"...and I yearned to be back with my wife and loved ones.

In a way, to the Christian, that's what life is. We build a world of love around our mate and our family and separation, even for a few days, brings sadness. But what we fail sometimes to realize is that beyond this life God promises even greater joy...a joy without death...a peace without pain. And our separation here in the sunset of years brings a glorious sunrise together with Him eternally! When once we see that other side all earthly glory will suddenly fade away.

Moses, assigning responsibilities, while in the Wilderness. By sharing his burden he was able to accomplish much more for the Lord.

Through many trials, God delivered Moses and his people from Egypt. There were some 600,000 men alone plus women and children. What a congregation! For 40 years he was to lead his people through the wilderness.

Before the Israelites reached Sinai, Jethro, the father-in-law of Moses, came to see Moses bringing with him Zipporah, wife of Moses, and their two sons.

When Jethro saw Moses working from early morning to evening acting as a judge hearing people's complaints, Jethro became concerned. Moses was 80 years old!

> *Why do you alone stand as judge...the thing that you are doing is not good. You will surely wear out...for the task is too heavy for you; you cannot do it alone.* (Exodus 18:14,17,18)

Jethro suggested he divide the work. Moses listened to him, accepted his advice, and appointed others to help him.

Many Pastors and Christian workers, unlike Moses, have not learned the technique of sharing their responsibility and as a result burn out physically at an early age. Moses did not retire at 80 but he realized his limitations and still accomplished much for the Lord until his death at 120.

Moses turned the leadership of the Israelites over to Joshua when Joshua was also about 80. Most people would have retired many years before eighty. But for Joshua and his friend, Caleb, this was not a time to retire...but a time to refire! Joshua supervised Israel's rituals (Joshua 5:2), and the construction of monuments (Joshua 4:4-7).

And who can forget Joshua's march of faith around Jericho for six days and its capture on the seventh day of blowing the trumpets! Then when five Amorite kings combined their armies for a united attack on Gibeon, Joshua came to the rescue of Gibeon. In faith he spoke to the Lord and commanded the sun to stand still (Joshua 10:12).

Moses, in his late years, learned how to divide his work. Joshua, in his late years, pressed on to greater challenges for God.

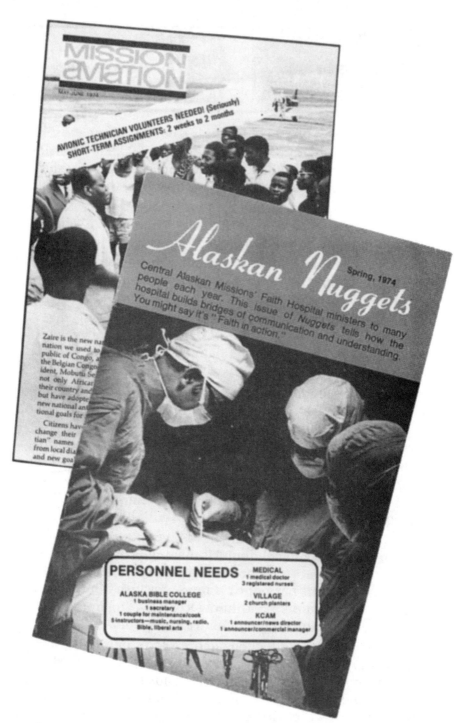

Look at your church literature rack. You will find many missionary bulletins such as the above. All need help desperately. Some missionary assignments are as short as two months or even two weeks.

Age is a quality of mind...if you've left your Dreams behind ...If hope is cold...If you no longer look ahead...If your ambitious fires are dead...Then, you are old!

Coming from a birthday party of a friend, Fred Allen was asked if the lady was old. "Was she old? When they lit all the candles on her birthday cake, six people were overcome with the heat!"

When a man has a birthday he takes a day off, but when a woman has a birthday she takes a year off!

No Christian should ever retire from the arena of God's ministry.

There does come a time when retirement from employment becomes a necessity. Suddenly you find yourself no longer getting up at 6 or 7 AM...going to work, meeting the challenges of the day...coming home at 6 PM, for a few hours of relaxation.

Suddenly the whole day is yours...and many people find they don't know what to do with it. They become withdrawn. Their marriage relationship withers. All the joy of living has disappeared. And although physically they are in good health, they waste away longing for death.

Don't fall into this trap of retirement. Keep yourself busy. Some, in their retirement years keep themselves busy around the house, painting, trimming, cutting the grass, planting. Others take time to travel. And all this is excellent. But, remember, what better opportunity do you have than in your retirement years to work for God.

Many missionary organizations would welcome your assistance. Many Christian colleges, churches could use your talents whether it is sweeping the floor or taking 5 or 6 months off to work in Alaska for Central Alaskan Missions building a hospital ward or in Africa setting up a bookkeeping system.

When you retire...REFIRE your life to spend more time giving back to God a portion of the wonderful years He gave you! And you will be healthier and happier for it!

Ahab, the seventh king of the northern kingdom of Israel (873-851 B.C.), married Jezebel and that's where his troubles began. Jezebel introduced the idolatrous worship of Baal into the kingdom. It was for this reason, the prophet Elijah proclaimed a drought upon Ahab's territory.

Three years passed and it was time for the drought to be broken. Elijah suggests a test with Ahab to see whether Jezebel's Canaanite Baal or the Israelite God is the true God. On one side would be 450 prophets of Baal plus the 400 prophets of the groves. All these false prophets were supported by Queen Jezebel. Just to feed these prophets would cost some $12,000 weekly in U.S. currency!

All 850 prophets are unable to bring fire from above to consume their offering. Elijah had reminded them that "...the God that answereth by fire, let him be God" (1 Kings 18:24). We all remember the story of how when Elijah prayed, in spite of the altar being soaked by water, God answered by fire and consumed the burnt offering (1 Kings 18:38).

When Ahab told Jezebel what had happened...she was very unhappy. John Barrymore said, "The way to fight a woman is with your hat...grab it and run!" And that's exactly what Elijah did...for Jezebel swore that before 24 hours had elapsed she would kill Elijah.

The next scene sees Elijah running. Here, Elijah, the mighty servant of Jehovah, with power to cause a 3 year drought and bring fire down from Heaven...is running...from a lone woman! What a comedown! Elijah was lonely, dejected... no one seemed to care. So exhausted, he rests under a juniper tree and prays: "Lord, take away my life; for I am not better than my fathers" (1 Kings 19:4). But God was not ready to take away his life. In fact Elijah has not even unto this day experienced death! (Perhaps a greater ministry awaits him as one of the Two Witnesses of Revelation 11 in the Tribulation Period???)

Elijah, after an angel fed him, hurried southward towards Mt. Horeb...180 miles from the place where he sat under a juniper tree. God then sent him back north about 300 miles. Elijah, so afraid of Jezebel, had not bothered to ask God for direction. Elijah, so dejected and alone reminds God: "I have been very zealous for the Lord; for the sons of Israel have forsaken Thy covenant...and killed Thy prophets with the sword. And I alone am left; and they seek my life, to take it away." (1 Kings 19:14).

But God reminds him he is not alone in 1 Kings 19:18: "Yet I will leave 7000 in Israel, all the knees that have not bowed to Baal...."

Elijah feels alone and dejected.

I don't believe I have met a more energetic man than Rev. Anthony Zeoli! You may know him as "the walking Bible," because of his ability to quote thousands of Scripture verses by memory. I took him on his first trip to the Holy Land when he was in his early 70's. He's pictured in the center of the photo in the light green shirt; my wife is in the blue sweater to the right. The scene is the Ascension Tower in Jerusalem. In your golden years take some time each year to travel, if you are able. Your life will be fuller for it.

Walter Winchell once said: "A real friend is one who walks in when the rest of the world walks out."

A friend is a jewel that shines brightest in the darkness. Your greatest social security is your friends. Win new friends but keep the old; the first are silver, the latter — gold! Friendship is the shadow of the evening, which strengthens with the setting sun of life.

If you spend your life building walls rather than bridges, then you have no right to complain when you are lonely.

Perhaps you remember reading in The Ancient Mariner:

I feel like one who treads alone
Some banquet-hall deserted,
Whose lights are fled, Whose garlands dead,
And all but he departed.

My wife Mary and I have 5 children. Two are now married. Occasionally our other three are out of the house either for a weekend or a special event...and we feel the pangs of loneliness. We realize someday all of our children will leave their nesting place. But we cannot allow our lives to sorrow in loneliness; rather to rejoice in the fact that we have a Saviour who reminds us: "...I am with you always..." (Matthew 28:20).

It must have been quite a lonely experience when Joshua, in his eighties, could no longer have the fellowship with Moses, his dear friend. But Moses reminded Joshua:

Be strong and courageous...the Lord is the one
who goes ahead of you; He will be with you. He
will not fail you or forsake you.

(Deuteronomy 31:7-8)

One reason for loneliness is that we do not know, in our older years, how to deal with time. We crawl into the shell of ourselves instead of becoming occupied with the will of God. The loneliest figure of all must have been Jesus Christ at Gethsemane. At Calvary He cried: "My God, my God, why hast thou forsaken me?" But God's presence sustained Him although the world had forsaken Him.

What about your loneliness? Have you brought it upon yourself. Visit as I have, the dying in the streets of Calcutta, the wretchedness of the plight of refugees on the burning sands of Jordan and you will be made to realize how fortunate you are. Dispel the sin of loneliness. Don't wait for others to come to you; go out and make friends. Offer your services, no matter how small, to your church, a Christian school or missionary organization. Be active in the Lord's work, as your health permits, and daily seek the comforting presence of God.

While Jesus prayed in Gethsemane His disciples fell asleep!

Have you ever wondered "What is man, that thou rememberest him? Or the son of man, that thou are concerned about him?" (Hebrews 2:6)

One day long before you and I were born, God, in the courts of Heaven, decided to send His son, Jesus Christ to earth! He was to be made a little lower than the angels. And though He was rich, for our sakes He was to become poor so that we through the poverty of Jesus Christ might become rich (Hebrews 2:9 and 2 Corinthians 8:9).

Even before He came to earth, He knew that those He came to save would mock Him and eventually place Him on a cross in Calvary.

Yet He was born in an obscure village in Bethlehem. There was no fanfare...except the stirrings of Herod who sought to kill Him.

For thirty years He devoted His time preparing for three momentous years. Satan tried to tempt Him in the wilderness (Matthew 4). His public ministry of helping others began at Capernaum. Shortly after that, by the Sea of Galilee, He called His first two of 12 disciples to follow Him, Peter and Andrew. To demonstrate His love and power He healed a centurion's servant, Peter's mother-in-law, a paralytic man, and many others. He cast out demons. He raised the dead.

When the Pharisees questioned him about eating with sinners He replied: "...I am not come to call the righteous, but sinners to repentance" (Matthew 9:13).

And all his disciples, for three years, witnessed His miracles, and all vowed allegiance to Him. They even followed Him to Gethsemane, but while Jesus prayed, they fell asleep! Then while one disciple betrayed Him, Peter became very brave and cut off one man's ear. As they took Jesus away to Caiaphas, the high priest, the Scriptures tell us:

Then all the disciples forsook him, and fled.
(Matthew 26:56)

When He needed them most...they fled! But the Lord recognized their weakness and though they forsook Him, He promises that He "...forsaketh not His saints; they are preserved forever" (Psalm 37:28).

175

Last year I watched as a bulldozer tore down an old stately white house to make way for an office building. It was like losing an old friend. What was once a home bustling with children was now a mass of rubble. Children would do well to remember that they too, one day will be old and they will yearn for the love of their children. New office buildings are nice but they can never replace the warmth of the old homestead.

I have met many people who in their retirement years are very lonely. In some cases, their children don't even visit them. I know of one dear saint in a nursing home whose only son has never visited her in years...yet they are just a few miles apart.

There is no greater demonstration of love than the love of God for us.

Can you imagine how the disciples who were so close to Jesus, who witnessed His miracles...would suddenly, in the midst of trials...run away and forsake Him. Yet Jesus not only loved them, He died to save them! He promises to preserve them forever! What love!

If He had so great a degree of love for us...should we not as Christians be an example of His love?

If our children do forsake us...even though we brought them into the world, fed them, clothed them, prayed them through many problems...should we be bitter and resentful?

Of course not. We should demonstrate the same love for them...even though they show no love...as Jesus Christ demonstrated for us! For only by exercising that love, will we have peace and happiness in our latter years.

Without the demonstration of that love, our latter years will be filled with envy, strife, remorse and loneliness!

My wife and I well remember the advice of a dear Pastor, George Mundell, who said, in effect: "Don't let the inconsiderate disposition of others affect yours."

Some children have left a godly home, gone out into the world tasting the temporary thrills of the world, and disowned their parents in the sunset years of life. But need it be sunset years? You can be old at 40 or young at 80. It all depends on your outlook on life. Stop feeling sorry for yourself. Count your blessings. When children forsake you, pray for them. God *does* answer prayer. Don't nag them. Don't say over and over and over: "Why don't you visit me?" Create an atmosphere of love in your home... so that they will *want* to come to see you with their children! Plan it so that when they do come it will be a time of joy in sharing...not despondency in caring!

Above all, follow the steps of Jesus Christ, who when He was bound and handed over to the high priest...when His own disciples deserted Him and fled...rested on the promises of His father for deliverance!

When Joshua fought with his army at Gibeon against the Amorites, he realized he needed more daylight to win the war. He asked the Lord for a miracle and he cried out: *"O sun, stand still at Gibeon, And O moon in the valley of Aijalon. So the sun stood still, and the moon stopped, until the nations avenged themselves of their enemies." (Joshua 10:12-13).*

The word "miracle" means a "marvelous event."

A miracle is an extraordinary event which cannot be explained in terms of ordinary natural forces. A miracle is often a sign or a token of a divine work. When performed by men of God, miracles confirm their call and mission from God.

There are over 80 miracles recorded in the Old Testament, and over 70 miracles recorded in the New Testament. But John tells us:

> And many other signs [miracles] truly did Jesus in the presence of his disciples, which are not written in this book. (John 20:30)

And then comes a very important verse that many people today overlook...supplying a major reason why Christ performed these miracles:

> ...these are written, that ye might believe, that Jesus is the Christ, the Son of God; and that believing ye might have life through His name.
> (John 20:31)

Christ did not perform miracles, however, solely to prove that He was the Saviour. He proved that He was the Saviour by doing the works of the Saviour. His miracle power was evidence of His omnipotence.

Whether He performed miracles while on earth or not would not have altered the fact that Jesus Christ was God. But He performed the miracles because He is God and He therefore often moves outside the scope of what we accept as natural phenomena. From His first coming to His last act on earth...they were beyond the ordinary course of Nature. Without any other evidence. His very coming to earth was a miracle!

Consider the following: (1) He was born of a Virgin, (2) His birth was announced by angels, (3) on the third day after His crucifixion He arose from the tomb in which He was buried, (4) He lived with his disciples for 40 days in a body superior to ours, and (5) He then, in the midst of over 500 witnesses, ascended to the Heavens and a cloud received Him out of their sight (Acts 1:9; 1 Cor. 15:6).

For any person, these miracles of Christ's life on earth should be sufficient proof that Christ is the eternal God. And yet the miracles He worked on earth were not done solely to prove Him God, but rather because He was and is God!

The mystery of creation is itself a miracle!

Does God work miracles today? Of course! And so does Satan!

And it takes a discerning Christian to filter out the chaff from the wheat.

Our responsibility as Christians is not to look for a miracle for our life. The miracle has already happened. Christ died for us. That's really a miracle. That we have "...passed from death unto life" (John 5:24), that's the ultimate of miracles!

Some Christians are like little children...always looking for another stick of candy. We have been bombarded by the false supposition that "something good is going to happen to you." As Christians it's about time we become less concerned about something good happening to us and be more concerned about something good (salvation) happening to those who know not Christ as personal Saviour and Lord. If only something good happens to us each day, then we should re-examine our Christian life. For when you are diligently working for the Lord, Satan will throw roadblocks in your path daily. If this is not the case, may I suggest "something good" may be happening because in your Christian testimony...NOTHING IS HAPPENING! Read how many times Paul was beaten and jailed...how a thorn in the flesh plagued him till the end of his life...which ended by beheading in a Roman dungeon! Only something good? Certainly not!

It would be a mistake to say that God does not work miracles today. But if miracles were regular occurrences, as many healing evangelists would have us believe, they would cease to be regarded as miracles. God in general ceased to work miracles at the close of the New Testament period. As He told Paul in 2 Corinthians 12:13 when Paul pleaded for his thorn in the flesh to be removed:

> *My grace is sufficient for thee; for my strength is made perfect in weakness. Most gladly, therefore, will I rather glory in my infirmities, that the power of Christ may rest upon me.*

Satan performs miracles. We seem to be seeing evidences of this today. And in the Tribulation Period...very convincing evidences will sweep millions into Hell. We are told in Revelation 13:13 that Antichrist's False Prophet "...performs great signs [miracles], so that he even makes fire come down out of heaven to the earth in the presence of men."

Christian...stop looking for miracle signs and start telling those who know not Christ about the miracle of redemption that occurred some 2000 years ago!

One playwright once wrote:

> Think not that anything can surpass
> the fury of a woman scorned.

There was no doubt about the fact that Queen Jezebel was mad...hopping mad! She was married to Ahab, King of Northern Israel. She was Syrian. And this unequal yoke alone was sin. Her father was also a priest of the Phoenician goddess, Astarte. The sacrifice of virginity at the temples was as an offering to Astarte. This coupled with Jezebel's worship of Baal, where human sacrifices were offered and licentious acts indulged, made Jezebel a fiery evil leader.

As soon as she became queen, she ruled. Ahab was king but he was completely under Jezebel's domination. (How many men do you know today who are ruled by their wives?) Jezebel ruled the king. She ruled the home. She ruled the nation. No one dared stand in her way.

Except Elijah. And he was the fly in her ointment!

Elijah condemned Ahab for marrying the wicked Jezebel and for furthering Baal worship to Israel.

Elijah prayed. God answered his prayer.

And for three years rain did not fall on the land. This further angered King Ahab and he attempted to slay all the Lord's prophets. During the drought Elijah was fed a little loaf of bread by the starving widow of Zarephath. The widow's sick son died. Elijah, in grief, carried the boy's body upstairs to the guest room, and he cried out to the Lord:

> O Lord my God, I pray thee, let this child's soul
> come into him again.

> (1 Kings 17:21)

God answered Elijah's prayer. The boy was brought back to life.

Then Elijah challenged King Ahab to a test to see who really was God, Jezebel's Baal or the Lord. All the people of Israel gathered at Mount Carmel along with 450 prophets of Baal and 400 prophets of Asherah. The God that answered by setting the altar of sacrifice afire would then be accepted as God. The prophets of Baal, despite all their earnest efforts, were unsuccessful. Elijah, to prove his point beyond a doubt, poured 12 buckets of water on the altar. Then Elijah prayed: "...O Lord, the God of Abraham, Isaac and Israel, today let it be known that Thou art God..." (1 Kings 18:36).

And God answered prayer! The altar suddenly became ablaze with fire!

Just as Jesus answered the prayer of Mary and Martha in bringing Lazarus back from the dead...Christ promises us an even greater answer to prayer...an eternal life with Him!

I must confess my prayer life is not what it should be! In this busy 20th century world we Christians simply do not take time to pray as we should. Oh, yes, we go through the perfunctory prayers.

And we too easily can fall into a routine of praying without meaning, praying without purpose...just because it is the thing to do.

It is not necessary that prayers be long or works of oratorical perfection. Nor, when we pray, must we suddenly modulate our voices to achieve a holy atmosphere...as some are in the habit of doing.

When Peter, trying to follow Jesus by walking on water, found himself suddenly sinking, he only had time to cry out a short prayer of desperation:

> Lord, save me.
> (Matthew 14:30)

And God answered prayer.

When Dorcas (Tabitha in Hebrew), an early Christian disciple living in Joppa, died, the family sent for Peter. Peter arrived and found all the women weeping around their departed loved one. He sent them all out, knelt down and prayed, turning to the body he said:

> Tabitha, arise.
> (Acts 9:40)

And God answered prayer. Peter presented her to the saints...alive!

I personally found...when I pray earnestly, seeking God's will, the answer comes quickly. When I've tried all other avenues...then suddenly I fall to my knees and cry out: "Lord, help me. I can't solve this problem myself. Guide me. Meet my need."

And He does! God does not give us everything we ask for. Because as James 4:3 reminds us, some things we ask for are requests from a selfish viewpoint.

To me prayer is like a telephone.

The telephone is always there in your home. But it only works when you pick up the receiver and dial a number. Then suddenly it becomes alive.

What has amazed me is that, when in sheer desperation I need help...I suddenly remember that telephone...God's telephone!

Perhaps you thought God had a private line...an unlisted number. Many Christians, by their life, would so indicate this. But God does have a telephone number. And it is listed. You will find it in Jeremiah 33:3:

> Call unto me, and I will answer thee, and show thee great and mighty things, which thou knowest not.

Could it be that you are going through the motions, by routine, perfunctory prayers, of dialing but not lifting up the receiver? Psalm 37:4 reminds us:

> Delight thyself also in the Lord; and He shall give thee the desires of thine heart.

To delight implies that what we are asking for is in keeping with God's will. It also implies that we are in a right spiritual state. If our lives are not what they should be as far as Christian service and dedication...then the telephone lines to Heaven will be corroded with rust...our fellowship with the Lord will become static.

To receive answers to our prayers we must: (1) Know Christ as personal Saviour and Lord; (2) forgive others who have offended us (Mark 11:26); (3) forsake known sin (Isaiah 59:1-2); and (4) we must pray in His will. Sometimes when one is insistent that God hear and answer a specific prayer, God will grant them that request as His permissive will as we read in Psalm 106:15:

> And He gave them their request;
> but sent leanness into their soul.

If it is consistent with the overall plan and will of God we are reminded in Psalm 50:15 to:

> Call upon Me in the day of trouble:
> I will deliver thee, and thou shalt glorify me.

Sometimes it is not His will. Paul prayed three times that God would remove his thorn in the flesh. But it was not God's will. But because of this thorn, Paul became a mighty warrior for God! God knew what was best for Paul in the long run—even though the thorn hurt for a while.

Have you ever seen a more descriptive picture of perfect faith? Would **you** have as much faith as this little chick?

The Lord tells us: *"...let us lay aside every weight...Trust in the Lord...and He shall give thee the desires of thine heart ...Rest in the Lord, and wait patiently for Him..." (Hebrews 12:1; Psalms 37:3,4,7).*

The Ark of the Covenant which was carried at the head of the march, through the miracle working power of God, was covered by a cloud by day and fire by night (Numbers 9:15-23). For 40 years their shoes did not wear out nor did their clothing get old! What a miracle! Have you ever worn a pair of shoes for even 10 years, let alone 40 years?

God wanted to teach His people of Israel some lessons. He sent them on a journey of 40 years in the wilderness of Sinai. Here were some 3 million people on a barren desert with no water and no visible means of support!

God provided everything...the endurance of their clothes, and their water and their food! After one year in the vicinity of Mount Sinai, the Israelites journeyed to Kadesh which is at the southern border of the Promised Land.

Before entering Canaan, Moses sent 12 men, one from each tribe, to spy out the land "...And see what the land is like, and whether the people who live in it are strong or weak, whether they are few or many. And how is the land in which they live, is it good or bad? And how are the cities in which they live, are they like open camps or with fortifications? And how is the land, is it fat or lean? Are there trees in it or not?" (Numbers 13:18-20)

After 40 days the scouting party returned and reported: "...We came into the land where you sent us; and it certainly does flow with milk and honey...nevertheless, the people are strong that dwell in the land...they are stronger than we...and we saw giants...and we were in our own sight as grasshoppers" (Numbers 13:27,28,31,33).

This should not have phased them! Here God had performed miracle after miracle in their lifetime, in delivering them from Egypt and in sustaining them in the desert. Yet what happened when the people heard this report?

> And all the congregation lifted up their voice,
> and cried; and the people wept that night...
> And all the children of Israel murmured...Would
> God that we had died in the land of Egypt!
>
> *(Numbers 14:1-2)*

Just eleven days from the land of promise! But they turned back! In eleven days they could have been in the Promised Land. Instead, because of their lack of faith, God made them spend 40 additional years wandering in the wilderness.

They did not pray, and their sin of worry brought them only increasing troubles!

Baby robin talking to young girl.

"Look at the birds of the air, that they do not sow, neither do they reap, nor gather into barns; and yet your Heavenly Father feeds them. Are you not worth much more than they? Therefore, do not be anxious for tomorrow; for tomorrow will care for itself..." (Matthew 6:26,34).

God is our refuge and strength, a very present help in trouble. Therefore will not we fear, though the earth be removed, and though the mountains be carried into the midst of the sea; Though the waters thereof roar and be troubled, though the mountains shake...The Lord of hosts is with us; the God of Jacob is our refuge (Psalm 46:1-3,7). Hallelujah!

There are many "swinging door Christians"—a lot of motion but getting nowhere! Are you one of them? Because the Israelites had a "grasshopper complex" God delayed His blessing to them for 40 years! How many blessings are you missing out on because you worry instead of trusting God in prayer?

We often sing the song: "Take your burdens to the Lord and leave them there." But somehow we can never leave them there. And somehow we just can't forget all about them.

A worry a day drains vitality away! Worry does not empty the day of its trouble but only of its strength! Worry is to life and progress what sand is to the bearings of perfect engines. Some people are such worry-warts that they worry that there is nothing to worry about.

Worry is like a rocking chair; it gives you the feeling of doing something, but gets you nowhere!

The atheist is one who believes there is no God; the man or woman who worries is one who lives as though there were none.

There are 773,692 words in the Bible but one will search in vain for a single occurrence of the word "worry" among them.

Dr. Oliver B. Greene likes to quote the following old poem:

> Said the robin to the sparrow,
>   I should really like to know
> Why these anxious human beings
>   Rush about and worry so.
>
> Said the sparrow to the robin,
>   I think that it must be
> They have no Heavenly Father
>   Such as cares for you and me.

When you worry, you doubt God's ability to answer your problem. And when you doubt God, you sin! Instead of worrying...you should kneel by your bed, tell God your problems and say, "Precious Saviour, here are the burdens of my heart. I am leaving them at your feet."

Dinah was the daughter of Jacob and Leah. Apparently she was a very beautiful girl.

One day she was sightseeing along the desert, away from the drab tents of her father. She wanted to see how the girls in nearby Shechem were doing. It was a typical neighborhood visit.

It was then that Prince Shechem, son of Hamor, spotted Dinah. And when he saw her:

> ...he took her and lay with her by force.
>
> *(Genesis 34:2)*

Shechem loved her and urged his father to arrange a marriage. King Hamor went to talk with Jacob about a marriage plan just as Jacob's sons came in from the fields. The sons were angry because Shechem "...had done a disgraceful thing in Israel by lying with Jacob's daughter, for such a thing ought not to be done" (Genesis 34:7).

Hamor pleaded: "The soul of my son Shechem longs for your daughter; please give her to him in marriage. And intermarry with us; give your daughters to us, and take our daughters for yourselves. Thus you shall live with us, and the land shall be open before you; live and trade in it, and acquire property in it" (Genesis 34:8-10).

Then Shechem pleaded as well and said if they agreed he would give anything to right the wrong, if only they would give him Dinah.

Jacob's sons had no forgiveness in their heart but used deceit and said:

> We cannot do this thing, to give our sister to one
> who is uncircumcised...Only on this condition
> will we consent to you; if you will become like us,
> in that every male of you be circumcised....
>
> *(Genesis 34:14-15)*

Hamor and Shechem both agreed and convinced their village to submit to circumcision. Three days later, however, when they were sore, two of Dinah's brothers, Simon and Levi, entered the town and killed every man including

Hamor and his son Shechem. They rescued Dinah and con-
fiscated all the flocks and herds and donkeys and took all
the women and children (Genesis 34:28-29).

Jacob was angry but the damage had already been done.

Simon and Levi, acting anxious that the heathen conform
to their law, used religion to promote their own wickedness instead of exercising godly love.

*Dinah's brothers slaying the men of Shechem in revenge
for the violation of their sister.*

Soon children grow up and if your love did not reach them in their childhood it will be more difficult to reach them as adults. Pictured are Doreen and Duane getting ready for their brother, Dennis' wedding to Eileen (whose photo appears to the right of Duane). Five years later, Doreen also got married. To all five of our children we strive to make our home life an example of Christian love.

The Scriptures tell us both:

> Children, obey your parents in the Lord; for this is right.

(Ephesians 6:1)

and,

> ...fathers, provoke not your children to wrath, but bring them up in the nurture and admonition of the Lord.

(Ephesians 6:4)

This does not imply that we should compromise our Christian testimony. But our life should be an example of Christian love. The oil of love will often calm troubled waters far better than the fire of law.

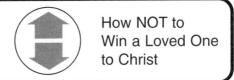
In the case of Jacob's sons...they claimed to be concerned with the covenant law of circumcision, but their later actions showed that they had no love. Perhaps they adopted the "holier than thou" attitude. They may have had short memories. Had Dinah not ventured into heathen Shechem to see the old world glamour...the massacre that followed could have been avoided. In fact, Josephus reports a tradition that Dinah went to the Canaanite annual festival of nature worship (Numbers 25:2). This was forbidden for an Israelite.

How many parallels have you observed today even in your own church? Have you witnessed Christians trying to win a loved one to Christ by making them adhere to certain standards, while they, themselves, overlook their own faults?

Some Christian parents are so busy in the Lord's work that they neglect their own children. Soon their children grow up. And the parents wonder where they went wrong when they see their children reject Christianity. Your missionary responsibility begins at home. If most of your nights each week are spent serving on committees in church or in some other church activity, then it is time you realign your priorities. I have seen many children go astray because their parents were too busy "serving the Lord."

Then, too, some parents forget that they, too, were once children! They become stern taskmasters. They will not bend. They set down plenty of laws for their children to follow, but exercise no love for their children to emulate. As a result, on the outside the children may out of necessity, obey. But when they get older the resentment of the growing-up years bursts into the open and they react by foolishly rejecting God. "If that's Christianity," they remark, "I want nothing to do with it."

And then, in old age, when the parents need their children's love and concern...they sometimes find that their own children neglect them and stay miles away. Sometimes bitterness goes so deep that the children will not even visit them as they lay dying!

God had a unique plan for Daniel's life.

At about 15 years of age Daniel was taken from Judah to Babylon in 605 B.C. (Daniel 1:1-6). He lived in Babylon throughout the entire 70-year period of captivity.

In Babylon he served under two entirely different powers:

Nebuchadnezzar Belshazzar }	Babylonian
Darius the Mede Cyrus }	Media-Persian

Nebuchadnezzar, king of Babylon, was the first Gentile world ruler to completely control the entire people of Israel, making Palestine an integral part of his domain. This was the beginning of "the times of the Gentiles" (Luke 21:24). It will end at the Second Coming of Christ (Luke 21:24-27). God sent Daniel to be prophet to both Gentile and Jew to show His sovereign will concerning all the nations of the world. This was a big job for Daniel. Yet, in spite of difficulties that were to face him...even the possibility of death...he showed both courage and faith.

Daniel was a man of strong purpose. He believed in living a clean, separated life. Nevertheless he was both wise and tactful. Although he would not eat the king's wine and food, he suggested a wise alternative (Daniel 1:8-14).

Daniel was a man who commanded respect and love even from many of his enemies. In public confrontations before kings he was brave. When Darius was deceived into signing a law that made it mandatory for all the subjects to worship the king's image, Daniel refused. For this Daniel was cast into the lion's den. Yes, Daniel, indeed was brave.

Yet, in spite of all his honor, he was modest and humble. He took no credit for himself but directed it to God (Daniel 2:28-30). Daniel was also a man of prayer. Knowing that the penalty for not worshipping the image of Darius meant being cast into a den of lions...Daniel did not compromise his position. He prayed to God.

Because of his vibrant testimony for God, "...the commissioners...began trying to find a ground of accusation against Daniel in regard to government affairs; but they could find no ground of accusation or evidence of corruption, inasmuch as he was faithful, and no negligence or corruption was to be found in him" (Daniel 6:4).

Because Daniel would not compromise God's standards his very life gained the respect of those who did not know the true God. His life became a mirror of God's undying love and grace.

Daniel, by his life, was a witness to both Nebuchadnezzar, the Babylonian king and Darius, the Mede.

(Circled pictures, left to right): Rev. Arthur Pryce, Mrs. Pryce, Salem Kirban, and Mrs. Kambeck.

This picture was taken August 25, 1940 at a Sunday School outing of a missionary church near Clarks Summit, Pennsylvania. Rev. Arthur Pryce was the Pastor of this small church held above a firehouse. An elderly couple, Mr. & Mrs. Ellison (now with the Lord), had enough interest in our family (we were on welfare) to take us to Montrose Bible Conference in Montrose, Pennsylvania every summer. There I accepted Christ as my Saviour and Lord.

But the seed was originally sown by the faithful ministry of Rev. and Mrs. Pryce, Mr. & Mrs. Ziegenfuss, the Kambecks and others, who by their life, showed me that Christianity was worth striving for. To them I shall be eternally grateful!

Montrose Bible Conference was started by Dr. Reuben Archer Torrey in 1908. As I stood at Torrey's mountaintop grave in the summer of 1974 I reflected on the legacy that his life generated. Sixty-six years ago when he started the Conference he had no idea how far reaching his testimony would be. Yet his life changed the lives of those you see pictured above. And their life, in turn, changed mine... eternally!

Concerning someone who is weak in the faith, you may have heard a leader remark: "Let's allow him to sing a solo in the Cantata, otherwise he will get discouraged."

By taking this type of action we often do not help the individual. Shielding him from problems...may contribute to his further downfall.

When someone comes to Christ he or she must realize that life will not be a bed of roses. Actually, because of this decision, greater problems may follow. If one is doing a real work for Christ, Satan will explore every avenue to break down that devotion.

Your life must be so full of love, devotion and such a pillar of strength in time of stress...that others, witnessing this, will want the same inner peace that you possess!

If men speak ill of you, live so that no one will believe them. Character is made by many acts; it may be lost by a single one. It was Shakespeare who wrote:

> The evil that men do lives after them,
> The good is oft interred with their bones.

Many times a person's entire Christian testimony is washed unceremoniously down the drain because of one misstep. In such cases, a Christian should acknowledge his sin, repent, and strive to again be an example. No Christian is perfect. And one thing that turns those who do not know Christ off is the fact that some Christians attempt to show they are superior.

You will not win a loved one to Christ if much of your life is spent on collecting material possessions for yourself. Nor will you be successful if you spend your time going to motion pictures or glued to a television set. For then, as far as your non-Christian friends are concerned, you will appear to be no different than them.

As 1 Peter 3:1-15 reminds us...we win others by becoming God's prime example of how accepting Christ can make us a new person...the type of persons others will want to aspire to become!

Many people, unfortunately, think life consists of earthly possessions. They spend all their lifetime collecting them... air conditioning, a swimming pool, two cars, a summer home at the shore or mountains...all possessions!

I have heard liberal clergymen scoff when you question them on Hell. They tell their congregations: "Hell is here on earth!" And by so deceiving them...they send their listeners straight to the pit of Hell!

Christ in Luke 12:16-21 reminds us about the rich fool. This man was so successful in his farming that his barns were overflowing. He couldn't get everything in. So, believing that money resolves all, he decided to tear down his barns and build bigger ones. Then he comforted himself by saying:

> ...Soul, you have many goods laid up for many years to come; take your ease, eat, drink and be merry.

But God told him:

> You fool! This very night your soul is required of you; and now who will own what you have prepared?
>
> *(Luke 12:19-20)*

The Lord tells us also about another rich man who was splendidly clothed and lived each day in mirth and luxury. One day a beggar, Lazarus, lay at his door and longed for a few scraps from the man's table. Eventually Lazarus died and he was carried by angels to be with Christ (Luke 16:22).

The rich man also died and was buried. But his soul went into Hell. There, in torment, he saw Lazarus in the far distance with Abraham. "Father Abraham," he shouted, "have some pity! Send Lazarus over here if only to dip the tip of his finger in water and cool my tongue, for I am in anguish in these flames" (Luke 16:24).

But Abraham reminded him that during his lifetime on earth he had everything he wanted; Lazarus had nothing...and it was too late to rectify the situation. Then the rich man pleaded with Abraham to at least warn his five brothers so they could avoid Hell. But Abraham reminded him that God's Word, our Bible, contains these warnings and they could read them anytime they want to.

But the rich man pleaded: "They won't bother to read them!" And Abraham made a very discerning reply: "...If they do not listen to Moses and the Prophets, neither will they be persuaded if someone rises from the dead" (Luke 16:31).

Lazarus asking for a few scraps of bread finds that only the dogs are his friends. This account illustrates the facts that: (1) no purgatory awaits the righteous; (2) one's destiny is settled in death; and (3) man's opportunity for salvation is NOW!

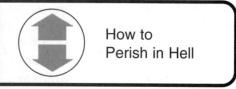
How to go to Hell?

It's easy!

Do NOTHING!   (John 3:18)

Just keep laughing along with the TV comedians who tell you "Well, if I go to Hell, I'll have a lot of company. All my friends will be there."

The closer I get to Christ the more revolting to me become the things of the world. I see how artificial they are. I have watched the late evening talk shows...watched the so-called stars parade in front of millions of viewers grasping for the height of popularity...and it's often like a re-run of Sodom and Gomorrah!

I have watched the TV giveaway programs, the soap operas and I have seen how they have warped the priorities of life in the hearts of men and women nationwide.

I have seen major networks devote one to three hours of prime time to bring to America rock concerts where drug-crazed youth spout out unintelligible ear-shattering sounds in the interest of "balanced programming." Those media personnel who are responsible for feeding this filth will have an eternity to answer for their error in judgment!

It is difficult to find many television programs anymore where sex does not ultimately become a major topic. It is not hard to predict that the X-rated motion pictures of the 1970's will be the accepted TV movies of the 1980's (or before)!

Most people don't want to talk about their future. Young people talk about getting an education. Those who have graduated from college talk about getting a job. Those who have jobs talk about getting ahead. Those who are ahead talk about retiring. And those who retire...are afraid to talk! Because the next step is DYING!

Suddenly all the years of scraping, stepping over other people, remodeling their home, building another home, buying two more cars, taking 3 more vacations to Miami, Acapulco or Tel Aviv...suddenly this does not mean anything anymore! They have come to the end of the road!

That's it! The glitter is gone. The glamour is gone! The jokes are gone! Their friends, for the most part are dead and gone! (As well as the comedians they watched). And there is nothing to laugh about. Hell becomes a reality! And by this time...so calloused they have become...that they fail to realize there **is an ANSWER** to eternal life. But they just can't believe it. So they do NOTHING. And by their inaction, they condemn themself to dying in their sins, in Hell...eternally!

One day the sands of time will run out for your life. Then... suddenly...in a split moment...it will be forever too late for you to choose Christ and eternal life with Him!

You have just read HOW TO LIVE ABOVE AND BEYOND YOUR CIRCUMSTANCES but if you have never accepted Jesus Christ as your personal Saviour and Lord...you can never resolve your problems.

The solutions offered in this book are of no value to you... until you first come face to face with life's greatest decision:

WHAT WILL YOU DO WITH JESUS?

Will you state that He never existed?

Will you simply say that He was a good man who did good things...like many other good men?

Will you say His message is not relevant to our enlightened age?

Your decision should not be based on what your friends or relatives say or do not say...or on your own private concept of heaven or hell. These really, in the final analysis, *do not matter!*

What is important...and what will govern your tomorrow in ETERNITY...is WHAT DOES THE BIBLE SAY? In light of God's standards, set forth in the Bible, your final destiny will be determined.

You can, as many do, simply choose to ignore Christ and the Scriptures...go on living your life, doing the best you know how to meet your problems, work to provide an income for your family, set aside a nest egg for retirement...

But THEN WHAT?

What happens when it comes time for you to depart from this earth?

Then WHAT WILL YOU DO WITH JESUS?

It takes NO DECISION on your part to go to Hell!

It **does** take a DECISION on your part, however, to go to Heaven!

> *He that believeth on Him is not condemned: but he that believeth not is condemned already, because he hath not believed in the name of the only begotten Son of God.*
>
> *(John 3:18)*

Whether you are Jew or Gentile, here are five basic observations in the Bible of which you should be aware:

1. ALL SINNED

   For all have sinned, and come short of the glory of God.

   (Romans 3:23)

2. ALL LOVED

   For God so loved the world, that He gave His only begotten Son, that whosoever believeth in Him should not perish, but have everlasting life.

   (John 3:16)

3. ALL RAISED

   Marvel not at this: for the hour is coming, in which all that are in the graves shall hear his voice.

   And shall come forth; they that have done good, unto the resurrection of life; and they that have done evil, unto the resurrection of damnation.

   (John 5:28,29)

4. ALL JUDGED

   ...we shall all stand before the judgment seat of Christ.

   (Romans 14:10)

   And I saw the dead, small and great, stand before God; and the books were opened...

   (Revelation 20:12)

5. ALL SHALL BOW

   ...at the name of Jesus every knee should bow...

   (Philippians 2:10)

Right now, in simple faith, you can have the wonderful assurance of eternal life.

Ask yourself, honestly, the question...

WHAT WILL I DO WITH JESUS?

Will you accept Jesus Christ as your personal Saviour and Lord or will you reject Him?

This you must decide yourself. No one else can decide that for you. The basis of your decision should be made on God's Word—the Bible.

A little boy, after mowing the lawn, ran into the kitchen and presented his mother with the following bill:

For mowing the lawn	$5.00
Sitting with baby brother	.50
Going to the store	1.00
Cleaning the attic	2.00
Weeding the garden	4.00
Taking out the trash	1.00
Total due me	**$13.50**

The mother, who was washing the dishes, dried her hands on her apron, turned the bill over and wrote this note:

I carried you in my womb. NO CHARGE!
I gave you life. NO CHARGE!
I nursed you when you were hungry. NO CHARGE!
I took care of your every need. NO CHARGE!
In the wee hours of the morning I rocked you to sleep in my arms. NO CHARGE!
When you were sick, I pleaded in prayer hour after hour for the Great Physician to heal you. NO CHARGE!
I have sacrificed all I have so you can have all I never had at NO CHARGE!
And even though you would disown me, I would do it all over again at NO CHARGE!
Because I love you

The boy, upon reading this, wrote on his bill **PAID IN FULL!**

What many of us seem to forget is that: God created

The Heavens   **NO CHARGE!**

The Earth   **NO CHARGE!**

The Universe   **NO CHARGE!**

The Waters   **NO CHARGE!**

The Plants
and fruit trees   **NO CHARGE!**

The Sun   **NO CHARGE!**

The Moon   **NO CHARGE!**

The Birds   **NO CHARGE!**

Every Living Creature

Then He brought forth Man ....**NO CHARGE!**

And for man He gave him Woman ....**NO CHARGE!**

Then God sent His Son to tell us of His
Father and to die for our sins ....**NO CHARGE!**

And all we have to do is to believe and
He promises to Give us Eternal Life at ....**NO CHARGE!**

And, now, for His saints, Christ is
preparing a mansion in Heaven for us at ....**NO CHARGE!**

How can I do less than give Him my best...and live for Him
completely **AFTER ALL HE'S DONE FOR ME!**

Jesus tells us the following:

> "...him that cometh to me I will in no wise cast out...
>
> Verily, verily I say unto you, He that believeth on me hath everlasting life"
>
> (John 6:37,47)

He also is a righteous God and a God of indignation to those who reject Him....

> "...he that believeth not is condemned already, because he hath not believed in the name of the only begotten Son of God".
>
> (John 3:18)

> "And whosoever was not found written in the book of life was cast into the lake of fire".
>
> (Revelation 20:15)

YOUR MOST IMPORTANT DECISION IN LIFE

Because sin entered the world and because God hates sin, God sent His Son Jesus Christ to die on the cross to pay the price for your sins and mine.

If you place your trust in Him, God will freely forgive you of your sins.

> "For by grace are ye saved through faith; and that not of yourselves: it is the gift of God:
>
> Not of works, lest any man should boast".
>
> (Ephesians 2:8,9)

> "...He that heareth my word, and believeth on Him that sent me, hath everlasting life, and shall not come into condemnation: but is passed from death unto life."
>
> (John 5:24)

What about you? Have you accepted Christ as your personal Saviour?

Do you realize that right now you can know the reality of this new life in Christ Jesus. Right now you can dispel the doubt that is in your mind concerning your future. Right now you can ask Christ to come into your heart. And right now you can be assured of eternal life in heaven.

All of your riches here on earth—all of your financial security—all of your material wealth, your houses, your land will crumble into nothingness in a few years.

206

And as God has told us:

"As it is appointed unto men once to die, but after this the judgement:

So Christ was once offered to bear the sins of many: and unto them that look for Him shall He appear the second time without sin unto salvation." (Hebrews 9:27,28)

THE CHOICE

Are you willing to sacrifice an eternity with Christ in Heaven for a few years of questionable material gain that will lead to death and destruction? If you do not accept Christ as your personal Saviour, you have only yourself to blame for the consequences.

Or would you right now, as you are reading these very words of this book, like to know without a shadow of a doubt that you are on the road to Heaven—that death is not the end of life but actually the climactic beginning of the most wonderful existence that will ever be—a life with the Lord Jesus Christ and with your friends, your relatives, and your loved ones who have accepted Christ as their Saviour.

It's not a difficult thing to do. So many religions and so many people have tried to make the simple Gospel message of Christ complex. You cannot work your way into heaven —heaven is the gift of God for those who have their sins forgiven by trusting in Jesus Christ as the one who bore their sin.

No matter how great your works—no matter how kind you are—no matter how philanthropic you are—it means nothing in the sight of God, because in the sight of God, your riches are as filthy rags.

"...all our righteousnesses are as filthy rags...." (Isaiah 64:6)

Christ expects you to come as you are, a sinner, recognizing your need of a Saviour, the Lord Jesus Christ.

HOW TO GET TO HEAVEN

I have met many well-intentioned people who feel that "all roads lead to Heaven." This, unfortunately, is false. **All roads do NOT lead to Heaven.**

All roads lead to DEATH...except ONE ROAD and ONE
WAY. Jesus Christ said:

> I am the door; by me if any man enter in, he shall
> be saved...
>
> *(John 10:9)*
>
> He that entereth not by the door into the sheep-
> fold, but climbeth up some other way, the same is
> a thief and a robber.
>
> *(John 10:1)*
>
> Thomas saith unto Him, Lord...how can we know
> the way?
>
> Jesus saith unto him, I am the way, the truth and
> the life: no man cometh unto the Father, but by me.
>
> *(John 14:5-6)*
>
> Take heed lest any man deceive you: For many
> shall come in my name, saying, I am Christ; and
> shall deceive many.
>
> *(Mark 13:5-6)*
>
> Neither is there salvation in any other; for there
> is no other name under Heaven given among men,
> whereby we must be saved.
>
> *(Acts 4:12)*

Many people feel they will get to Heaven through the
teachings of Bahai, British-Israelism (Armstrong),
Buddhism, Christian Science, Jehovah's Witnesses, Mor-
monism or some of the mystic cults of India or Japan.
But all these roads will lead you directly to Hell!

There are not many Teachers. There is ONE Teacher, the
Lord, Christ Jesus! There are not many roads. There is
ONE ROAD...the Lord, Christ Jesus. The Bible warns us:

> But though we, or an angel from Heaven, preach
> any other gospel unto you than that which we
> have preached unto you, let him be accursed.
>
> As we said before, so say I now again, If any man
> preach any other gospel unto you than that ye
> have received, let him be accursed.
>
> *(Galatians 1:8-9)*

Understanding this, why not bow your head right now and
give this simple prayer of faith to the Lord.

Say it in your own words. It does not have to be a beautiful
oratorical prayer—simply a prayer of humble contrition.

My Personal Decision for CHRIST

"Lord Jesus, I know that I'm a sinner and that I cannot save myself by good works. I believe that you died for me and that you shed your blood for my sins. I believe that you rose again from the dead. And now I am receiving you as my personal Saviour, my Lord, my only hope of salvation and eternal life. I know that I'm a sinner and deserve to be condemned at the judgment. I know that I cannot save myself. Lord, be merciful to me, a sinner, and save me according to the promise of Your Word. I want Christ to come into my heart now to be my Saviour, Lord and Master."

Signed ....

Date ....

If you have signed the above, having just taken Christ as your personal Saviour and Lord...I would like to rejoice with you in your new found faith.

Write to me...Salem Kirban, SECOND COMING/*Missions*, Box 276, Clayton, Washington 99110...and I will send you a booklet to help you start living your new life in Christ.

HOW TO LIVE ABOVE and
BEYOND YOUR CIRCUMSTANCES!

Now that you have read this book, you have two options:
1. Put it aside as an interesting book;
2. Put the advice to work in your own life.

This book cannot answer all your problems. Nor, in reality, can it answer <u>any</u> of your problems until you first acknowledge Jesus Christ as your personal Saviour and Lord.

In my travels I find many Christians who get bogged down by the PROBLEMS in their life. And I have always offered them this one GOLDEN COMMENT. It is a rule, that if people could really grasp and practice, would save a lot of needless heartache:

Don't tell me your problem! WHAT IS THE SOLUTION?

Look into your own life. Have you become so unhinged stewing and brewing over your problem? Why?

> *The Lord's hand is not shortened, that it cannot save; neither His ear heavy, that it cannot hear.*
> *(Isaiah 59:1)*

Don't ever waste your time worrying about the problem! All this action can give you is sleepless nights, rob you of the joys you would have with your children, rob you of communion with your mate, perhaps a bad case of shingles, heart skips, irritability, nervousness, a short temper, physical and perhaps mental exhaustion...and most tragic of all ...separate you from the fulfillment of God's love and contribute to Satan's pleasure. That's what constant worrying will do!

What will worrying <u>NOT</u> do? <u>It will NOT solve your problem!</u> Therefore, if worrying will NOT solve your problem... why worry?

What will solve your problem? The SOLUTION! In other words, <u>don't look at the problem...SEEK THE SOLUTION!</u> Worrying will not solve your problem...but seeking the solution to your problem will solve your problem!

Now I realize this sounds simple. Yet, let's consider it for a moment!

Our daughter, Doreen Frick, with Jessica. Jessica has Hemangioma. Doctors who are specialists say the best treatment is **no** treatment. After the first 18 months the body's regenerative and healing processes start to work and by about six years of age, in many cases, healing is complete. The natural healing processes of our body are a miracle in themselves!

Let's take a personal example.

In the beginning of the book I mentioned our grand-daughter, Jessica, was born with Hemangioma, a benign tumor of the blood vessels. As I look at her, her right eye greatly swollen and shut, I wish I could take her place. My wife, our daughter and son-in-law are all greatly concerned. And this is as it should be. They, and I, feel the pain of this illness. Yet, in God's wisdom, Jessica is unaware of this affliction.

That's the problem...Jessica has Hemangioma. Now, should we spend our time worrying about the problem. We have... to be honest with you, we are human. Yet, through this problem, the Lord has helped us not to become consumed in worry...but rather to seek the *solution* to the problem.

In our case our solution is two-fold:

1. Commit Jessica to the Lord, first! And seek His wisdom and ask God, if it be His will, to perform a miracle of healing in her life;
2. Give her the advantage of the best in medical advice and treatment.

We have done both...and because, at this writing, Jessica's condition remains the same and perhaps even a little more aggravated, we are continuing this two-fold solution to the problem. Her parents, Wes and Doreen, have taken Jessica to the best eye-doctors, radiologists and plastic surgeons in the Philadelphia area. Their advice: wait and let nature take its course for a few more months.

And I must admit...to wait is hard! It is especially hard on the parents, when inquisitive people gaze at the distorted face of a little 4 month old child...it simply breaks their hearts.

Still, as Christians, we must not worry by becoming overwhelmed by the problem. We must seek the solution!

And the solution is not a neatly cut answer all the time.

Now, if you have just been laid off from your job. You can do two things:

1. You can worry and fret about how you are going to pay your bills;

or

2. You can seek the SOLUTION and *start looking for another job* and pray: "Lord I am leaving this in your hands. Guide and direct me."

But suppose you have just come from the doctor's office and he has told you that you have cancer. Now the solution is not as simple...or is it?

1. You can worry and fret...but all the worry about the problem will **NOT** resolve the problem;

    or

2. You can seek the solution!

    Cancer can give you a negative attitude in your life...even towards the Lord.

    If you have cancer

    A. Thank God for the new opportunities that this will give you to witness for Christ;
    B. Thank God that it is an absolute truth that all who trust in Christ have eternal life (John 11:25-26);
    C. Adopt a positive attitude of joy in witnessing for Him during this time;
    D. Ask God to work a miracle of healing in your life, if it is His will.

And as He passed by, He saw a man blind from birth. And His disciples asked Him, saying, "Rabbi, who sinned, this man, or his parents, that he should be born blind?"

Jesus answered, "It was neither that this man sinned, nor his parents; but it was in order that the works of God might be displayed in him."

(John 9:1-3)

Every problem has a solution! But that solution is not always the solution we seek. God may allow us to become ill. That's a problem. Our solution is that we get better. But that is not always God's solution. He may want us to witness for Him while ill, and then to join Him in Heaven for joys so great our human hearts cannot fathom. Initially, we may not think this is the solution. And yet when we meet Him, we say, Lord how could we have been so foolish!

For I consider that the sufferings of this present time are not worthy to be compared with the glory that is to be revealed to us.

(Romans 8:18)

Do you remember something...anything that you really wanted badly in life? You tried everything to get it. But God blocked the door. At the time you were bitter. But now as you look back you say, "How I thank God He did

214

not allow me to have my will."

For every problem...God has a solution...so why worry. It may not be *your* solution. But if you know God's Word, you can rest assured that His solution will be the best solution for you and for your loved ones. It is beyond our human understanding.

So, we get back to the original concept. This book is not meant to be the answer to your problems. It is only meant to make you aware of your circumstances by showing you that in Bible days others had similar circumstances. The problems you face are not peculiar with you. Nor will they end with you.

> *And we know that God causes all things to work together for good to those who love God, to those who are called according to His purpose.*
>
> *(Romans 8:28)*

This book should merely be the starting point where you praise God for your problems...cease to worry...and seek the Holy Spirit for the solution!

WE MUST START BELIEVING!

One dear friend of mine had two of her children nearly die because of illness in their youth. She herself had 5 operations. She tells of one operation...while she was on the operating table, in danger of dying, her physician had to plead with the surgeon to come in off the golf course to perform emergency surgery. And now her husband, in reasonable good health, for the past 3 years has become a recluse, rarely leaving his home.

All these sorrows and more she has been able to bear, but then one daughter married an unbeliever! And this has been her most difficult cross to carry. Why? Her daughter knows Jesus Christ as her personal Saviour. She grew up in a Christian church. Why would God allow this union to occur?

This dear friend is a dedicated Bible teacher...knows the Scriptures far better than I...yet this trial, quite naturally, has caused her much worry.

It is easy for me to tell others not to worry. I realize this. Yet, I must emphasize the fact that if worry will not get us anywhere except further away from God...then we must stop worrying and start believing! We must start believing

No one can serve two masters;
for either he will hate the one and love the other,
or he will hold to one and despise the other.
You cannot serve God and Mammon
[riches; see Luke 16:9,11,13].

For this reason I say to you, do not be anxious for your life, as to what you shall eat, or what you shall drink; nor for your body, as to what you shall put on. Is not life more than food, and the body than clothing?

Look at the birds of the air, that they do not sow, neither do they reap, nor gather into barns; and yet your heavenly Father feeds them. Are you not worth much more than they?

And which of you by being anxious can àdd a single cubit [18 inches] to his life's span?

And why are you anxious about clothing? Observe how the lilies of the field grow; they do not toil nor do they spin.

Yet I say to you that even Solomon in all his glory did not clothe himself like one of these.

But if God so arrays the grass of the field, which is alive today and tomorrow is thrown into the furnace, will He not much more do so for you, O men of little faith?

Do not be anxious then, saying, "What shall we eat?" or "What shall we drink?" or, "With what shall we clothe ourselves?"

For all these things the Gentiles eagerly seek; for your heavenly Father knows that you need all these things.

But seek first His kingdom and His righteousness; and all these things shall be added to you.

Therefore do not be anxious for tomorrow; for tomorrow will care for itself. Each day has enough trouble of its own.

(Matthew 6:24-34)

His Word when He says:

...being justified by faith,
we have peace with God...
we glory in tribulations also,
knowing that tribulation worketh patience...

(Romans 5:1,3)

My brethren, count it all joy when ye fall
into various trials, Knowing this, that
the testing of your faith worketh patience...

(James 1:2-3)

Paul, in thanking God for his thorn in the flesh said:

Therefore, I take pleasure [am well content] in
infirmities, with insults, with distresses, with
persecutions, with difficulties for Christ's sake;
for when I am weak, then am I strong.

And He said unto me, My grace is sufficient for
thee; for My strength is made perfect in
weakness...

(2 Corinthians 12:10,9)

And look at this:

...I will never leave thee, nor forsake thee.

(Hebrews 13:5)

Do you know what the original Greek is for this verse just quoted? Here it is! God was actually telling us:

I will positively not leave you, and I will positively
not forsake you.

(Literally: "I will not not leave you, and I will not not forsake you" — the double negatives represent the strongest possible denial in the Greek language.)

What greater promise than this could we as Christians ever want or hope for?

Did you know these verses existed? Probably so. But perhaps you had a head knowledge of their existence...now make it a HEART KNOWLEDGE. Appropriate these promises for your life...right now!

Go to your bedroom or quiet place. Take out a sheet of paper. (Or use the one in the back of this book.) On one side write down all your problems. Actually write them down. I sincerely mean this. Actually take the time to physically write down each and every problem.

Spell it all out so it is there before you.

On the other half of the page (on the other side of the sheet) ...after you have enumerated your problems...write the word

GOD

That's all!

Fold the paper in such a manner that the word GOD covers the problems you have written.

Then pray...asking God to give you wisdom...and in His way, to bring about the solutions to your problems. Take your burdens to the Lord.

THEN LEAVE THEM THERE.

At night, take that piece of paper. Put it under your pillow. And sleep on your problem...resting in Christ Jesus. Don't think or mull over the problem in your mind. But simply say, as your head hits the pillow: THANK YOU DEAR JESUS FOR DYING FOR ME. THANK YOU...THANK YOU. Let your problem be His problem, and let this be the stop sign that directs your lips to PRAISE. And God will do the rest.

You will then have learned the secret of HOW TO LIVE ABOVE AND BEYOND YOUR CIRCUMSTANCES.

If this book is used by God to help you, please write me. It would thrill my heart.

Thank you Lord for giving me the words to write this book. My prayer is that it may be a blessing to the person who has just finished reading it... that he or she might learn to live above and beyond circumstances...in Christ Jesus.

Salem Kirban, SECOND COMING/*Missions,*
Box 276, Clayton, Washington 99110

GOD

...we know that God causes all things to work together for good to those who love God, to those who are called according to His purpose.
(Romans 8:28)

...I will never leave thee, nor forsake thee.
(Hebrew 13:5)

FOLD with this copy **IN**

MY PROBLEMS
(List briefly in 4 or 5 words)

1. _____

2. _____

3. _____

4. _____

5. _____

6. _____

7. _____

I believe God is able to resolve **all** my problems and I this day commit each and every one to His care.

_____ _____
Date   Write your Name

My MISSIONS Gift Response Form

Enclosed is my Gift to spread the Good News of Christ's
soon return. **Send Christian Growth Helps below.**

ORDER NUMBER	DESCRIPTION	FOR A GIFT OF
_____	_____	$_____
_____	_____	$_____
_____	_____	$_____
_____	_____	$_____

Why not order EXTRA copies of HOW TO LIVE ABOVE & BEYOND YOUR CIRCUMSTANCES and give to a loved one. This book makes an <u>excellent</u> Gift!

☐ 1 copy / $15   ☐ 3 / $25   ☐ 7/ $35

$_____

$_____

$_____

Total Enclosed $

☐ Check or money order enclosed in the amount of $_____ payable
to **SECOND COMING, Inc.** [U.S. funds only].   Sorry, no C.O.D.'s.

☐ **VISA** [| | | | | | | | | | | | | | | | |]
Expiration Date ☐☐☐

☐ master charge [| | | | | | | | | | | | | | | | |]
Expiration Date ☐☐☐

Signature X_____

Mr/Mrs/Miss_____
[Please PRINT]

Address_____

City_____State_____ZIP_____

SECOND COMING/*Missions*   Your Gift is Tax Deductible
Box 276, Clayton, Washington 99110 U.S.A.

For <u>any</u> Size Gift to SECOND COMING _Missions..._

Each month you give...you _automatically_ receive a copy of the current issue of _WORLDWIDE NEWS !_

Personally written by Salem Kirban.

Worldwide News is a confidential newsletter that covers current world events as they relate to the fulfillment of Bible prophecy.

Each month's issue reveals how close we are to the soon coming Rapture!

This is concise news analysis you will not read elsewhere! Don't miss this unique opportunity be an informed Christian!

WORLDWIDE NEWS

is sent *automatically* each month to those who support
SECOND COMING / *MISSIONS*.   My wife, Mary, and I
founded this non-profit ministry in **1970**.   It is a literature
ministry.   The purpose: To distribute Bibles and books on
Bible prophecy to seeking souls around the world.   Your
Gift to this ministry **is** tax-deductible!

THE KIRBAN REPORT

is sent *automatically* each month to those who support
my wife, Mary and me, *personally*.   Our desire is to not take
funds from **Second Coming/Missions** for our personal
support, when possible.   **The KIRBAN REPORT** is sent
monthly to those who send us $5, $10, $15 or $20 or $25
monthly for our <u>personal support</u>. This Gift to us <u>personally</u>,
of course, is **not** tax-deductible.   I cover prophetic news
events that I cannot write in a non-profit publication.

SPECIAL EDITION KR / 11-02

A Confidential Newsletter to Supporters of Salem & Mary Kirban ministries

CONGRESS
IS AN EXPERT ON
PORK BARREL POLITICS

The KIRBAN REPORT
Salem Kirban's <u>personal</u> analysis
of current world affairs as they
relate to the <u>soon coming</u>
RAPTURE!

The United States is in very, very bad shape
financially.   Yet, in spite of our economic
chaos the President is ready to spend some

PORK BARREL...when used to describe
a bill, implies the legislation is loaded with
special projects for Members of Congress to

The
KIRBAN REPORT

The KIRBAN REPORT is a confidential Newsletter written by **Salem Kirban**

It is <u>automatically</u> mailed each ~~~th to those

HOW TO DISCOVER THE SECRET
OF WHO CONTROLS THIS WORLD

If you want to know who controls the world...**FOLLOW THE MONEY TRAIL !**
And if you want to know who controls those who <u>manipulate</u> those who use
money as a wedge to accomplish their own evil ends...then go to your Bible and
read **Ephesians 6:10-12**.

How It All Began...

Since **1970**, **SECOND COMING/Missions** has been distributing the Word of God worldwide by way of the printed page. My interest in Bible prophecy began in **1938**. As a young child I attended a little missionary church in Clarks Summit, Pennsylvania. [Clarks Summit is a small town about 10 miles above Scranton]

Church services were held in a rented room on the 2nd floor of the Fire Hall in the center of town. Rev. Pryce was the Pastor. It was here my brother, Lafayette, my sister Elsie and I were brought to church each Sunday.

The photograph **below** was taken in **1938** at the annual church picnic at Covey's Farm in Clarks Summit. I am that little boy in the circle on the front row. I can remember vividly at this picnic the various church members discussing the book of Revelation and prophecy. And, remember, this was **1938**! This discussion was the first spark that kindled a flaming desire for me to understand God's prophetic promises better.

And it was from this beginning that eventually led me to start **SECOND COMING/*Missions*** in **1970**. My desire was to make sure that Bibles and books on Bible prophecy would be available to seeking souls worldwide. By your faithful giving...you are making this dream come true...year after year!

WHAT IS SECOND COMING/*Missions*?

SECOND COMING, Inc. is a Non-Profit ministry dedicated primarily to printing Bibles and prophetic portions of Scripture for <u>FREE</u> distribution throughout Asia, Africa, the Middle East and the far unreached areas of the world.   Salem Kirban is President of **SECOND COMING, Inc.** This Non-Profit global ministry began in 1970.

Salem Kirban is the author of over 50 books including GUIDE TO SURVIVAL, 666, YOUR LAST GOODBYE, THE RISE OF ANTICHRIST, SATAN'S MARK EXPOSED and COUNTDOWN TO RAPTURE.   He and his wife, Mary, have 5 children...Dennis, Doreen, Diane, Duane and Dawn.   All but one is married.   Diane is in full-time Christian service.

SECOND COMING/Missions Began In JERUSALEM
125,000 Copies of GUIDE TO SURVIVAL
Mailed Throughout All Of ISRAEL

When Mary and I began **SECOND COMING/*Missions*...**I traveled around the world on a one-month journey.   My first stop was Vietnam, where, as a war correspondent, I reported on the Vietnam War.   I also stopped in Korea, Thailand, Cambodia, India and finally ended up in Jerusalem.   The 6-Day War was just ending and I witnessed Arab refugees pouring out of Israel towards Jordan.   As an Arab myself... [because my parents were born in Lebanon]...I had a heart of compassion for their plight.

And as a <u>Christian</u> Arab, I also realized the challenge to reach the people of Israel with the good news of eternal life.   And that's how **SECOND COMING/*Missions*** began...by arranging with a missionary in Israel to translate **GUIDE TO SURVIVAL** into <u>Hebrew</u>.   This book was printed right in Jerusalem.   Over a 3-year period we printed **125,000** copies of **GUIDE TO SURVIVAL** and mailed them direct to Jewish people <u>throughout all of Israel</u>.   The response was wonderful...and that's how **SECOND COMING/*Missions*** began its literature ministry of Bible distribution throughout the world.

In this Catalog...we make available to you CHRISTIAN GROWTH HELPS so you can better understand Bible Prophecy and God's Plan for you from the Rapture all the way up to the eternal New Heavens & New Earth. We are **not** in the business of selling books and cassettes.   We <u>ARE</u> in the ministry of <u>getting out the Word of God worldwide.</u> Therefore, when you send a Gift to SECOND COMING...we are happy to provide you with items in this Catalog to help you grow spiritually.   And by your generous giving...you help this ministry reach out to lost souls worldwide.

NOW! Completely Updated, Revised and ENLARGED!

by Salem Kirban

432 Pages!
36 Chapters!
56 Feature Pages!

Over 100 ILLUSTRATIONS and CHARTS!

Sometime in the near future several Million people will suddenly **disappear!** They will vanish *"in the twinkling of an eye."* That's why this book was written originally in 1968. But current world events are shaping up to complete chaos! Germany is reunified! The Common Market nations are uniting as one major force with a common currency! Russia is holding up her deceptive dove of peace. The Middle East is a powder keg . . . ready to explode into a World War. **That's why I have completely updated, revised and ENLARGED** this _new_ edition of **GUIDE TO SURVIVAL.**

Some of The Exciting Chapters That Tell HOW THE WORLD WILL END!

Guide To Survival
How Current News Events Reveal Shocking Fulfillment of Prophecy.

Power That Destroys
How the Nations of the World Now Have An Arsenal of Death.

The Vanishing Christians
How Christians Will Be Raptured and How The World Will React.

Russia's Rise To Ruin
How Russia and her allies, including Germany, will invade Israel!

Is Antichrist Alive Today?
Why The Time Is Ripe For Antichrist To Prepare His Entrance!

Miracle Worker and Executioner
How The World Is Already Welcoming A Coming False Prophet!

Lulled Into A False Security
How People Will Willingly Accept The Mark **666**! Much more!

The Day of Terror and Tragedy
The **21** Tribulation Judgments and the terror that follows.

The Battle of Armageddon
The Monumental Death Toll and the Amazing Miracle That Occurs!

If you want to know what is going to happen in the near future you want to make sure both you and your loved ones get *GUIDE TO SURVIVAL.* The last chapter is a Decision chapter pointing the reader to Christ. Leave this book in a prominent place in your home so it serves as a constant witness even after you have been raptured.

GUIDE TO SURVIVAL   **Yours for a Gift of $25**   **Order No. 261**

The Day of the MARK is already here!

- Soon you will need it to:
- Cash your Social Security check!
- Withdraw money from your Bank!
- Enter a Hospital! • Buy Food!

SATAN'S MARK EXPOSED

by Salem Kirban   Photos & Charts

HERE ARE THE 20 REVEALING CHAPTERS

SPECIAL FEATURES Include

1 Automatic Identification Systems
2 Your Television Set...a Spy Network!
3 Supermarket Lasers Endtime Sign
4 How MARK May Be Applied
5 Controlling You by Satellites!
6 Who Will Be The Antichrist?
7 What Will Be His MARK?
8 Your Worldwide Money Card!
9 **5** Ways Antichrist Will Control!

LASER IDENTIFICATION BEAM

Your banks have already installed sophisticated devices that can **deny** you the right to withdraw **your own** money! Not even your Safe Deposit Box will be sacred! "Smart" credit cards with a tiny memory chip [smaller than a dime] will contain your entire life history...reduce you to a number!

To Receive	SATAN'S MARK EXPOSED	
One Copy	For a Gift of $25	Order No. 8

666 The Best Selling novel by **SALEM KIRBAN**

If you liked **LEFT BEHIND**...you will love this exciting novel on the Tribulation Period written by Salem Kirban in **1970**. It covers the **Rapture** and the climactic events of the **Tribulation Period**. The events Salem Kirban wove into his novel were unheard of at that time. Now, over **30** years later they are becoming a stark reality!

---

15 SUSPENSEFUL CHAPTERS in **666**

1 I Saw The Saints Rise	**8** Secret Flight To Babylon
2 The Great Reassurance	**9** Startling Pronouncement
3 The Sinister Plot	**10** Search For Safety
4 Flight To Moscow	**11** The Shocking Spectacle
5 Cloud of Death	**12** The Strange Destroyer
6 Invasion From North	**13** The Sound of Death
7 Triumph and Tragedy	**14** March On Megiddo

And I saw the souls of those who had been beheaded because of the testimony of Jesus and because of the Word of God, and those who had not worshiped the beast or his image, and had not received the mark upon their forehead and upon their hand, and they came to life and reigned with Christ for a thousand years [Revelation 20:4]

One of **24** illustrations in **666**. Plus another feature is that many pages also include corresponding Scripture text. This is not just a novel, but a learning experience in Bible Prophecy.

TO RECEIVE 666   For a Gift of $25   Order No. 4

If you want to know what **HEAVEN** will be like...then order this book. It is a sequel on **HEAVEN** by **SALEM KIRBAN**. Use Order Form at the back of this book.

WHEN TIME
SHALL BE NO MORE

1 Copy / $15   3 copies / $25

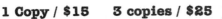

233

WHAT IN THE WORLD WILL HAPPEN NEXT ?

By SALEM KIRBAN

☐ 28 Chapters ☐ 350 Pages ☐ Fully Illustrated

This book ranks among the most vital witnessing books to reach the world for Christ! It answers in one book every crucial answer to life's eternal destiny! Why not give to loved ones and friends.

SALEM KIRBAN Answers Life's 5 Most Important Questions...

WHAT IN THE WORLD WILL HAPPEN NEXT ?
At last! Here is a, clear, step by step explanation of the sequence of the **14** events that are **yet to occur** on God's Timetable! A page is devoted to each event...from the **Rapture** to the **New Heavens and New Earth**! And that's not all. There is a pictorial description of all **21** Tribulation judgments.

WHAT IS LIFE?
Answers such questions as: Why did God create you? What is your purpose on earth? What is the meaning of life on this earth? Since your life span is under 100 years...what are your most vital priorities in light of an eternity? Are the things you consider important really important?

WHAT IS THE RAPTURE ?
One of these days MILLIONS will suddenly DISAPPEAR from this earth without any warning "...*in the twinkling of an eye*." This is called **The RAPTURE** ! The Bible tells us that no one knows the day nor hour. However, God does give us clear indications of what to look for just before His coming for His saints! **We are now in that Time Period!**

WHAT IS HELL?
Is there a real Hell? Is there real torment? Where is Hell? Is Hell a place of consciousness? Is it a place of darkness? What are the greatest torments one will suffer in Hell? Where are the unsaved dead before their Judgment Day? How can one escape an eternity of life in Hell? Must that decision be made while one is alive?

WHAT IS HEAVEN?
You will find the answers to such questions as: What is life like in the 1000 year Millennium? Do our loved ones who are already in Heaven know what is happening on earth now? What type of body will we have in Heaven? Will we recognize our loved ones in Heaven? How do we become immortal? Where is Heaven? Revealing Charts and Photos!

To Receive	WHAT IN THE WORLD WILL HAPPEN NEXT?	
One Copy	For a Gift of $15	Order No. 282
Three Copies	For a Gift of $25	Order No. 283

Dear Friend of
SECOND COMING/*Missions*,

Mary and I believe the **PRINTED** WORD is the most effective...most lasting...and the least expensive way to tell others that *CHRIST IS COMING AGAIN... SOON !*

That is why
SECOND COMING/*Missions*
is dedicated to getting out the Gospel by way of the printed word! **SECOND COMING** is a *worldwide* missionary organization. We have a **7-point** ministry outreach. **Your faithful monthly Gift will help us win souls for Christ!**

Salem **and** Mary

From Our Heart To Your Heart

① **ISRAEL** / *"...To the Jew first..."* [Romans 1:16]. Our first priority is to Israel. **Second Coming** has printed 125,000 copies of **GUIDE TO SURVIVAL** in Hebrew in Jerusalem and mailed them throughout all of Israel.

② **WORLD EVANGELISM** / This ministry has helped in the support ofNationals and missionaries both at home and throughout the world.

③ **BIBLE DISTRIBUTION** / This is a primary ministry of **SECOND COMING/*Missions*.** We ship Bibles free to seeking souls in Africa, Asia, the Middle East and the unreached areas of the world! [Isaiah 5:11]

④ **COMFORT and COUNSELLING** / Many of those who support this ministry have burdens and heartaches. Mary and I share in these concerns both by prayer, personal letters of encouragement and practical help.

⑤ **PROPHETIC CONFERENCES** / We have conducted over **400** prophetic conferences in Churches throughout the United States including Alaska!

⑥ **NATURAL HEALTH** / We help ailing missionaries and Christian workers giving them Scriptural guidelines for abundant health.

⑦ **CHRISTIAN GROWTH HELPS** / SECOND COMING mails each month thousands of copies of our Prophetic Newsletters and books...to those who support this ministry.

Those who support **SECOND COMING/*Missions*** monthly receive *Salem Kirban's* **WORLDWIDE NEWS** which ties in current events with Bible prophecy.

This **Salem Kirban REFERENCE BIBLE** was first published in 1979. It went out of print in July, **2002**! In order to get the cost per copy in line for a **2000 page FULL COLOR Bible**...the printing cost to reprint **15,000** copies is **$225,000** !

Our ministry's annual income is less than **$295,000** a year! I have contacted several major Christian publishers and none are interested in reprinting the Bible. One publisher told me:

"BIBLE PROPHECY IS NOT '*IN*'".

This Bible has **10** *exclusive* features that no other Bible has! There is Commentary on every page. Also included are Time Period Symbols. P*lus* the book of Revelation has **360** pages...and all these pages are printed in Full Color with complete Commentary on each page!

Some who are reading this page can give $1000, $5000 or $10,000. Perhaps there is one person who can give the entire amount: $225,000. You are investing in souls won to Christ! What better investment is this than God's Holy Word. You will reap Crowns in Heaven for your faithfulness!!

YOUR GIFT...sent now...will help our **BIBLE REPRINT FUND** to reprint this **FULL COLOR**, **2000** page Bible. Send your ,Gift, large or small, to:

SECOND COMING/*Missions*, Box 855, Loon Lake, WA 99148. Your Gift is Tax-Deductible!

My MISSIONS Gift Response Form

Enclosed is my Gift to spread the Good News of Christ's soon return. **Send Christian Growth Helps below.**

ORDER NUMBER	DESCRIPTION	FOR A GIFT OF
_____	_____	$_____
_____	_____	$_____
_____	_____	$_____
_____	_____	$_____
		$_____
		$_____
		$ _____

Why not order EXTRA copies of HOW TO LIVE ABOVE & BEYOND YOUR CIRCUMSTANCES and give to a loved one. This book makes an excellent Gift!

☐ 1 copy / $15 ☐ 3 / $25 ☐ 7/ $35

Total Enclosed $
_____

☐ Check or money order enclosed in the amount of $_____ payable to **SECOND COMING, Inc.** [U.S. funds only].   Sorry, no C.O.D.'s.

☐ **VISA** | | | | | | | | | | | | | | | | | |

Expiration Date ☐☐☐

☐ master charge | | | | | | | | | | | | | | | | | |

Expiration Date ☐☐☐

Signature X_____

Mr/Mrs/Miss_____
[Please PRINT]

Address_____

City_____State_____ZIP_____

SECOND COMING/Missions   Your Gift is Tax Deductible
Box 276, Clayton, Washington 99110 U.S.A.